The Cult of Sincerity

THE CULT OF
SINCERITY

Herbert Read

HORIZON PRESS
NEW YORK

First published in the United States of America 1969
by Horizon Press, 156 Fifth Avenue,
New York 10010

© *The Herbert Read Discretionary Trust 1968*

Library of Congress Catalog Card Number:
69-11931

Printed in Great Britain

Preface

The essays in Part I of this volume are concerned with my 'sincere' attempt to express a personal philosophy. The more particular essays in Part II express my indebtedness to some of my contemporaries, but, alas, they are incomplete. My debts are indeed multifarious, and with as much justification I might have included essays on, say, Alfred North Whitehead, Wilhelm Worringer, Ernst Cassirer, Martin Buber, Karl Mannheim, C. F. Ramuz and Albert Camus. The influence of these writers may not always be evident or acknowledged, but as in the case of Jung and Eliot, the direction of my thoughts would have been different if I had not encountered them, either in person or through their writings. What they have in common is perhaps difficult for others to discern, but whatever it may be it is sufficiently indicated for me by this word 'sincerity'. Of all of them we may say with Coleridge: So he *is*, so he *writes*, and that, as I said in *The True Voice of Feeling*, is the principle of all my criticism.

H.R.

Contents

Acknowledgements

These essays have appeared previously in various publications, but most of them have been revised or elaborated for this volume. The following are the details:

(1) *The Cult of Sincerity*. THE HUDSON REVIEW.

(2) *The Truth of a Few Simple Ideas*. THE SATURDAY REVIEW OF LITERATURE, February 18, 1967.

(3) *What is There Left to Say?* ENCOUNTER, XIX, October, 1962.

(4) *Apology for E.S.* Hitherto unpublished.

(5) *My Anarchism*. ENCOUNTER, XXX January, 1968

(6) *T. S. Eliot: A Memoir*. THE SEWANEE REVIEW, Winter, 1966. Also printed as a pamphlet by the Wesleyan University Press, Middletown, Connecticut (1966) and in T. S. ELIOT: THE MAN AND HIS WORK, London (Chatto & Windus), 1967.

(7) *Carl Gustav Jung*. Part (*i*) THE SUNDAY TIMES, June 11, 1961, with additions. *Part* (*ii*) hitherto unpublished.

(8) *The Early Influence of Bertrand Russell:* A contribution to BERTRAND RUSSELL: PHILOSOPHER OF THE CENTURY, edited by Ralph Schoenman, London, Allen & Unwin, 1967.

(9) *Richard Aldington*. A contribution to RICHARD ALDINGTON: AN INTIMATE PORTRAIT (eds. Alister Kershaw and Frédéric-Jacques Temple), Southern Illinois University Press, 1965.

(10) *D. H. Lawrence*. Elaboration of an article that appeared originally in WORLD REVIEW, July, 1950.

(11) *Edwin Muir*. ENCOUNTER, XII, 1959, with additions.

PART I

I

The Cult of Sincerity

One can never know one's own life,
or rather there is almost always
something within us which does not
wish to become aware of itself.
JEAN GUÉHENNO: *Jean-Jacques Rousseau*

(i)

Sincerity! All my life I have been reproved for attempting to use this
word, and rightly so because the very notion of sincerity implies a
consciousness of one's self as a circumscribed entity, a 'single one'
(Kierkegaard) or a 'unique one' (Stirner), to be defined and defended, and that state of self-consciousness is itself insincere. What
then is sincere?—perhaps only an unwitting naivety: the naivety of
a child before it has eaten of the fruits of the tree of knowledge and
still lives in an unreflecting state of innocence. Some rare geniuses
may be able to recall a momentary awareness or retain a memory-
trace of that state and then endeavour to establish its existence in
their own hearts and minds—Traherne and Blake are examples
from English literature, but even their innocence is suspect. The
very consciousness of innocence is at the same time a consciousness
of experience. We may make the distinction and cultivate innocence;
but such a conscious decision is sophisticated and therefore no
longer sincere.

Rousseau is the high priest of this cult and the undying fascina-
tion of his *Confessions*, *Reveries* and *Dialogues* lies in the fact that all

these autobiographical writings are attempts to define and defend a
self. An attempt to define sincerity might be sincere but the word
definition implies a fixed outline, seen from a particular point of
view. For this reason Rousseau criticized Montaigne, his great
predecessor in the cult of sincerity: he had painted himself only in
profile. Rousseau tried hard to avoid that limitation, but he did not
succeed—his *Confessions* were abandoned at the point where they
became too tormenting to himself, too insincere. It is true that he
had succeeded in making 'a clean breast' (our English idiom is very
expressive) of those 'sins' which had haunted him all his subsequent
life—the false witness he bore against a servant-girl when she was
charged with a theft he had himself committed and the abandonment of his five children to the foundling hospital—but again it
must be pointed out that the confession of sins is not necessarily an
act of sincerity: it is not a disinterested act and in any case Rousseau
did not make a public confession—his *Confessions* were not published during his lifetime. In his introduction to the *La Pléaide*
edition,* which is now the best available, Marcel Raymond points
out that the classical prototype of all confessors, Saint Augustine,
again confines himself to the sins of his youth, and that his object is
not so much to reveal a man (himself) 'dans toute la vérité de la
nature' (Rousseau's famous phrase in the opening paragraph of his
Confessions) but to reveal a sinner who turns towards God for
forgiveness, and is therefore more concerned to know God than to
know himself. The revelation is of the self as sinner, the self in
an attitude of contrition, desiring absolution. Rousseau, too, never
escapes from this self-regarding attitude of abnegation, and much as
he intends to be 'absolutely' sincere, his good intention is not
achieved because, as M. Raymond points out, his pride compels him
to prevaricate, even to lie. He cannot rid himself of the conviction
that his true self is naturally innocent, and that his sins were in some
sense acts of insincerity. He did not—rather, by his very nature,
could not—commit a sin sincerely.

What, then, is sincerity? 'Yours sincerely' is now in English the

* Paris (Gallimard), 1959.

14

commonest formula for concluding a letter—that is to say, the most insincere. And yet no other word expresses so well the rectitude, the exactitude we aspire to in presenting ourselves to the world. Ours is an age of confessions—never were so many autobiographies and autobiographical novels written, published and read by an eager public. Rousseau himself would not have revealed (or committed) the enormities expressed in the confessional writings of Céline, Miller, Genet, Burroughs and many others. And yet are these writings 'sincere'? Gone, of course, is any claim to natural innocence; these writers would rather boast of their natural depravity and claim the virtue of courage for their self-exposures. But compared with Rousseau (or Augustine or Montaigne) their confessions end by boring us. This may be partly a question of style: Rousseau was a superb artist: every sentence vibrates with passion and restraint. Our modern writers do not know the meaning of restraint (*mesure* in expression), with the result that their phrasing is crude and repetitive, their structure fragmentary, their tone devoid of eloquence. Such literary values they might condemn as 'insincere', so again we return to the question we began with—what is sincerity?

In an early work* I declared that 'the only thing . . . indispensable for the possession of a good style is personal sincerity' and I associated (in several places) sincerity with passion. 'Those who would persuade us of the truth of a statement must rely, not on an air of conviction or a show of reason, but on the compelling force of an emotional attitude.' Rousseau would have agreed with such an irrational doctrine, but its pragmatic truth depends on the word 'persuade'. Equally, there is equivocation in the word 'good'—a good style is not necessarily a precise style—the whole art or science of rhetoric is involved. The real question is the effectiveness of a particular style for a particular purpose, a question which Bonamy Dobrée and I analysed in *The London Book of English Prose*.† If the particular purpose is confessional, we may with justice demand 'personal sincerity'. Sincerity is then closely related to passionate

* *English Prose Style*, London (Bell), 1928.
† London (Eyre & Spottiswoode), 1932.

conviction. Confession is not self-analysis, in any clinically objective sense. Confession naturally takes the form of a narrative—a narrative about oneself. 'Moi seul. Je sens mon coeur et je connois les hommes.' But *sentir son coeur* is a privilege only granted to the exceptional man—the one who has the ability to find words that exactly (or, *to himself*, convincingly) express his feelings.

His feelings as they flow spontaneously from his contacts with nature and with man. Since each individual is unique, his feelings will be peculiar to himself, and he must find the exact words to express this peculiarity. He is sincere in the degree of the exactitude of this equation. Feeling comes in aid of feeling, as Wordsworth said: the feeling for the value of the words helps to define the feeling itself. That is what I mean by sincerity, but I do not wish to disguise the difficulty, and the rarity, of the process. The common failure is to allow habitual words and phrases, flowing spontaneously from the memory, to determine and deform the feelings. The whole exercise is one of exquisite perception and instinctive judgement.

(ii)

On several occasions I have drawn attention to the writings of an American psychologist, Ernest Schachtel, on childhood amnesia. Why do we forget our childhood? With rare exceptions we have no memory of our first four, five, or six years, and yet we have only to watch the development of our own children during this period to realize that these are precisely the most exciting, the most formative years of life. Schachtel's theory is that our infantile experiences, so free, so uninhibited, are suppressed because they are incompatible with the conventions of an adult society which we call 'civilized'. The infant is a savage and must be tamed, domesticated. The process is so gradual and so universal that only exceptionally will an individual child escape it, to become perhaps a genius, perhaps the selfish individual we call a criminal. The significance of this theory for the problem of sincerity in art (and in life) is that occasionally the veil of forgetfulness that hides our infant years is lifted and then we recover all the force and vitality that distinguished our first experiences—the 'celestial joys' of which Traherne speaks, when the eyes feast for the first time and insatiably on the beauties of God's creation. Those childhood experiences, when we 'enjoy the World aright', are indeed sincere, and we may therefore say that we too are sincere when in later years we are able to recall these innocent sensations. Such moments of re-vision are momentary, but their very rarity makes them significant (makes them aesthetic) and our works of art are given their essential vitality by successive injections of this primary experience.

All this has been described beautifully, intimately, even scientifically in Proust's great novel, whose very title, *A la recherche du temps perdu*, reveals the secret motive of all art—at least, of all art that is 'music', in the sense that memory, as the Greek myth has it, is the mother of the muses. We need no other theory of inspiration, especially if we take account of the all-inclusiveness of the child's curiosity. 'Everything is new to the newborn child. His gradual grasp of his environment and of the world around him are discoveries which, in experiential scope and quality, go far beyond any discovery that the most adventurous and daring explorer will ever make in his adult life. No Columbus, no Marco Polo has ever seen stranger and more fascinating and thoroughly absorbing sights than the child that learns to perceive, to taste, to smell, to touch, to hear and see, and to use his body, his senses, and his mind. No wonder the child shows an insatiable curiosity. He has the whole world to discover'.* These are the sensations and feelings that are gradually blunted by education, staled by custom, rejected in favour of social conformity.

Included in this childhood experience are not only sensations in the normal sense—sights and sounds, tastes and smells, graspings and gropings—but the first hearing of words, the first association of a particular word with a particular thing, the word itself *as a thing*. Poetry is nothing but the recovery of that magical experience. We

---

* Ernest G. Schachtel: *Metamorphosis*, New York (Basic Books), 1959, p. 292.

may use words to describe events, to express thoughts, to establish reality, but their peculiar poetry is derived from the associations they have with our childhood experiences, when we first discover that things have names, and that these names fit them with poetic justness.

If this equation of poetry and primal vision is accepted, we may abandon the very concept of sincerity: it is no longer necessary as an aesthetic value. But it survives as a moral value, and that is the sense in which we apply it to confessional writing. That, through all the mental prevarications of the *Confessions*, is Rousseau's concern: to assert the supreme moral value of native feelings of innocence. Similarly, Blake's *Songs of Innocence* celebrate the moral value of innocence, but they are not themselves innocent—they are very sophisticated. All art is artifice, and therefore no work of art is sincere. Once we become conscious of a feeling and attempt to make a corresponding form, we are engaged in an activity which, far from being sincere, is prepared (as any artist if he is 'sincere' will tell you) to moderate the feeling to fit the form. The artist's feeling for form is stronger than a formless feeling. Art is the definition, the delimitation, of feeling. To quote a powerful image of Stravinsky's (in *The Poetics of Music*) the lava is already cold by the time it has assumed a form. When we recognize feeling in a work of art, it is not the artist's feeling: it is our own feeling transferred to a ready form. A work of art is a feeling in-formed.

That is why it is possible for art to reconcile inner conflicts. So long as the inner drives, motives, passions involved in a conflict (and thereby constituting a psychosis) remain undefined, it is not possible to resolve the conflict. The conflict is, however, resolved by means of a symbolic form, a unitary structure in which conflicting forces are reconciled. Not all art is tragic, but tragedy is the highest form of art and the paradigm of its reconciliatory function.

(iii)

Sincerity, we may conclude, is a moral and not an aesthetic virtue, but all activities may be subjected, *ab extra*, to moral judgement. About this 'subjection' there has been much confusion in our time, of political and specifically Marxian motivation. The extreme point of view, now (in the autumn of 1966) being asserted in the Chinese Republic, is in effect an apothesis of moral judgement. Not even Kierkegaard could have made such a complete separation and subordination of the aesthetic judgement. The Russian politicians, especially during the Stalinist period, condemned the non-committed artist, and above all an artist like Pasternak who dared to use his art critically. Abstract art was condemned, not so much because it was 'pure', but rather because it was associated with the art of the bourgeois west, and was therefore reactionary. Art should be 'in the service of the revolution', and in that sense it should be 'proletarian'. But in spite of the introduction of new 'types' and new 'situations', proletarian art remained essentially the same as the academic art of the bourgeoisie. The difference between Sholokov and Tolstoy, or between any Soviet painter and any Tsarist painter, is not an aesthetic difference. The more Soviet art strove to be different, the more it remained the same thing.

The Chinese now have the ambition to create a totally new kind of art, breaking abruptly with their 'traditional' art, which they preserve for historical reasons, and in which they even take a nationalistic and possessive pride. But revolutionary art, Maoist art, is to be something quite different. We wait for any convincing manifestations of this new art, and meanwhile may conclude that it too, the more it strives to be different, the more it will remain the same thing.

Art remains the same thing because human nature remains the same thing—a 'thing', a fact of nature, socialized, civilized, domesticated, but not changed in any basic sense from prehistoric times. Art, as I have often argued, is not only a civilizing agency (the 'order' of society being an aesthetic concept, as Plato argued); it is also a progressive agency, in that it can modify (direct, concentrate, focus) human sensibility. The organism remains the same—the same nervous system, the same recording brain—but it is 'tuned' to a different pitch, and this pitch determines our ability to create a 'world vision', that is to say, 'the whole complex of ideas, aspirations and feelings which links together the members of a social group (a group which, in most cases, assumes the existence of a social class) and which opposes them to the members of other social groups'.* It is such a world vision, original and opposed to the world visions of the capitalist past, that the Chinese are endeavouring to create. But it is a mistake to assume that they can do it by any other means than those which have created the world visions of the past—the refinement and focussing of the aesthetic sensibility through the agency of the artist. The artist is not a different kind of man—he is a 'prole' with the rest of struggling humanity—but he has a particular sphere of work (the creation of *works* of art, symbolic structures, myths) and he specializes in certain techniques—poetry, painting, sculpture, music—with the aim of linking together 'the whole complex' of ideas, aspirations and feelings that gives meaning to the life of the community. Those ideas, aspirations and feelings are vague and formless until the artist comes along with his in-forming techniques. But these techniques, though made perfect by practice, are not determined by social or political aims. They are technical skills: part of a human being's acquired physical and mental equipment. The pick may be transformed into a ploughshare and finally be driven through the soil by a tractor, but the purpose remains the same—to turn the unchanging sod. All the inventions that constitute man's 'progress' do not change the essential purpose of the instrument nor the material it cultivates. In the same way, the structure of society may change, the methods of production and distribution; but the function of the work of art does not change, nor its means, nor its methods; it is an instrument for tilling the human psyche, that it may continue to yield a harvest of vital beauty.

---

* Lucien Goldmann, *The Hidden God*, London (Routledge & Kegan Paul) 1964, p. 17.

(iv)

I return to the problem of sincerity. Though we must admit that it is a moral rather than an aesthetic virtue, I am still conscious of the fact that all sincere confessions are invariably works of art, and this is not so much a question of their form, which may be rambling, but of their style. But what is style? Yeats (in *Ideas of Good and Evil*) speaks of 'the continuous indefinable symbolism which is the substance of all style', and explains that 'All sounds, all colours, all forms, either because of their preordained energies or because of long association, evoke indefinable yet precise emotions, or, as I prefer to think, call down among us certain disembodied powers, whose footsteps over our hearts we call emotions; and when sound, and colour, and forms are in a musical relation, a beautiful relation to one another, they become, as it were, one sound, one colour, one form, and evoke an emotion that is made out of their distinct evocations and yet is one emotion'. This we might take as an elaboration of Schachtel's theory, for what can those disembodied powers be but buried sensations of sound, colour, and form that have retained, ready for release, all their pristine vigour, their 'preordained energies'? The deliberate act (or action) of recall, if successful, reanimates those long forgotten associations, in all their 'continuous, indefinable symbolism'.

The symbolism is indefinable because it has been formulated in the unconscious, that region of the mind where buried memories associate and marry, drawn together by their sensuous affinity or 'musical relation'. It is true that a writer's style is not always, and even not often, formed by the effort of recollection. Rousseau wrote his various Discourses and *Le Contrat Social* before he even contemplated his *Confessions*, and most autobiographies have been afterthoughts of a busy career. But if Schachtel is right and if I understand Yeats properly, every kind of writing that is not rational and enumerative is in some sense metaphorical, or, as Yeats would prefer to say, symbolical. He mentions, not only beautiful lines that are easy to remember, but also 'some line that is quite simple, that gets its beauty from its place in a story, and see how it flickers with the light of the many symbols that have given the story its beauty, as a sword-blade may flicker with the light of burning towers'.

In support of these general observations is the curious fact that some of the most beautiful autobiographies have been written by men (and women) of an unpoetical nature. I am using 'unpoetical' in its technical sense, meaning writers not capable of poetic composition. I will not include among these one of the most beautiful autobiographies in any language, John Ruskin's, for much of his prose, like Pater's, is poetic in all but formal arrangement. Carlyle is not poetical in this sense, though he has great eloquence; but his reminiscences of his father and of his wife, Jane Welsh, are symbolical in Yeats's sense: they flicker, if not with the light of burning towers, at least with the glow of a consuming remorse and self-pity. But it is time to draw a distinction between those autobiographies that are merely narrational, and keep to the surface of events, such as those of Gibbon and John Stuart Mill, and those that are confessional, in the sense already defined, such as those of Rousseau, De Quincey, Amiel, Newman, Tolstoy, Jung. The problem of sincerity does not arise in the case of Gibbon or Mill; they aim to be truthful, which is not the same. Gibbon, of course, is occasionally eloquent, as in the famous passage describing his emotions on completing the *Decline and Fall*; but Mill's *Autobiography* is, as Sir Leslie Stephen complained, almost wholly lacking in the qualities which give charm to that class of literature. Even Harold Laski, a great admirer of Mill, who quotes this complaint in his Introduction to the World's Classics edition of the *Autobiography* (1924) admits that 'even his most intimate friends are judged much as a writer would judge a person whose obituary estimate he had been charged to compile'. And this was a deliberate policy on Mill's part: he wished his narrative to be unemotional, objective. That might even be his conception of sincerity.

Psychoanalysis has made us all suspicious of 'the objective truth'. We know now that it is a construction of the intellect (of the superego, as Freud calls it) and though such a truth may be socially viable, and even indispensable for the maintenance of a certain way of life, of the fabric of a civilization we have slowly elaborated from generation to generation, it is not the whole truth, for the whole truth is subjective, and only to be represented symbolically. But the question for the autobiographer is whether this subjective truth can be represented in any other way—or, to be more specific, objectively. Can the truth as Rousseau wished to present it be expressed in the style of Mill? For that matter, could Mill have reconciled any truth about himself with a 'System of Logic'? A genuine difficulty for any rationalist, as we see in this passage from the *Autobiography*:

'I also resumed my speculations on this last subject (Logic), and puzzled myself, like others before me, with the great paradox of the discovery of new truths by general reasoning. As to the fact, there could be no doubt. As little could it be doubted, that all reasoning is resolvable into syllogisms, and that in every syllogism the conclusion is actually contained and implied in the premises. How, being so contained and implied, it could be a new truth, and how the theorems of geometry, so different in appearance from the definitions and axioms, could be all contained in these, was a difficulty which no one, I thought, had sufficiently felt, and which, at all events, no one had succeeded in clearing up'.

Except, perhaps, the author of *Alice in Wonderland*. Mill, as he confesses, took to the poetry of Wordsworth as an escape from the syllogism. Wordsworth alone, for 'compared with the greatest poets, he may be said to be the poet of unpoetical natures, possessed of quiet and contemplative tastes. But', Mill admits, 'unpoetical natures are precisely those which require poetic cultivation'.

There is a distinction here between poetry and truth, or poetry and experience, and most people, however unconsciously, maintain such a distinction. A conflict arises when the poet would be truthful, as Wordsworth tried to be in *The Prelude*. But we know that he was not truthful in this confessional poem—he suppressed, or disguised, important events in his life. He himself knew that he had not succeeded in his aim, and shortly after completing it (in 1805)

23

confessed to Sir George Beaumont that the day of its completion 'was not a happy day for me; I was dejected on many accounts, when I looked back upon the performance it seemed to have a dead weight about it, the reality so far short of the performance . . . '* This may only be the common reaction that comes to any conscientious author on completing a work and comparing the outcome with the first intention, but he did not allow the poem to be published until 1850 and in the intervening years tinkered with the text in a manner which shows that his dissatisfaction was not merely textual, but concerned the substance and truth of his confession.

In addition to his *Confessions* Rousseau wrote, late in his life, three dialogues to which he gave the title *Rousseau Juge de Jean Jaques*. It is a very curious and significant work, and comes to the heart of the problem we are discussing. Rousseau separates himself into two selves, the self he was born, his true self, and the self he has been compelled to become by circumstances, and above all by the calumnies and subterfuges of his enemies. It is perhaps the same distinction that the modern psychologists make between the persona, the confident self we present to the public, the mask we wear, and the self beneath the mask, sensitive and diffident and subject to self-doubt: the ideal self and the real self. Most autobiographies present the ideal self and do so without any intentional deception. In English we do not habitually make the French distinction between *amour-propre* (self-respect) and *amour de soi* (self-love). Self-respect degenerates into pride, self-love into selfishness or egotism, but Rousseau is concerned to affirm the child-like innocence of self-love and its divine origin in the love of God. Wordsworth too, in his *Ode:*

> Heaven lies about us in our infancy!
> Shades of the prison-house begin to close
> Upon the growing Boy . . .

The Youth still is 'Nature's Priest'

* *Early Letters of William and Dorothy Wordsworth*. Ed. by Ernest de Selincourt. Oxford, 1935, p. 497.

> And by the vision splendid
> is on his way attended;

but then:

> At length the Man perceives it die away,
> And fade into the light of common day.

But Rousseau does not see this progress as a natural development, but rather as a gradual perversion of innocence. In the character of Rousseau he speaks of Jean Jaques in these terms (Deuxième Dialogue):

'Of all the men I have known the one whose character derives most clearly from his temperament is J.J. He is as nature made him: education has only slightly modified him. If at the moment of his birth his faculties and energies had developed suddenly, from that time onwards one would have found him almost as he was in his maturity, and now after sixty years of trials and tribulations, time, adversity and men have still not changed him much. Whilst his body has aged and is broken, his heart remains ever young; he retains the same tastes, the same passions that he had in his younger days and until the end of his life he will never cease to be an old child.'

Rousseau's purpose, therefore, in his *Confessions* was to establish the inevitability (and therefore the innocence) of the course of his life. He became what he was, in the sense of the command: Become what thou art! His end was in his beginning, and the beginning was innocent. It is true he had committed sins, but he could explain why such an innocent nature as his had been led to commit them, and of course he would not have committed them if circumstances had not been against him. Even that most heinous sin, the sending of his five children one after the other to the foundlings' home, could be explained away as a sacrifice for their real benefit: he had neither the means, nor the ability, to give them a better upbringing. Rousseau pretended that he had been forced to abandon his children by Mme Le Vasseur, the mother of the woman who lived with him for thirty-three years, from 1745 until his death in 1778. But he does not explain why he could not have abandoned Mme Le Vasseur instead of his children. Presumably Thérése would not allow him, and there is no doubt about his commitment to her—as we may see from his letter to Mme. de Luxembourg dated 12th June 1761:

'I did not marry the mother, nor was I in any way obliged to do so, since before we lived together I told her that I would not marry her; in any case, a public marriage would have been impossible because of the difference of religion; I have, nevertheless, always loved and respected her as my wife, because of her kindness of heart, her unparalleled unselfishness, and her absolute fidelity—in respect of which she has never given me the slightest cause for suspicion.'

It has been pointed out by Jean Guéhenno that during his lifetime Rousseau never admitted the truth about his children, and when questioned, he lied. 'The admission is to be found only in works which were to be published after his death.' So much for his sincerity, then! But M. Guéhenno also points out that there can be no doubt that Rousseau regretted this 'sin', and that his work is in many respects 'his rumination on his remorse'. *Emile* in particular would not have been written, or written with so much force and feeling, had he not been brought to consider the rights of children in contemplation of the wrongs he had committed against his own children—'he was only able to explain what was right because he knew what it was to have done wrong.'*

'Yes, Madame, I put my children in the Foundlings' Home; I entrusted them to the institution whose function it is to provide such support. Since my poverty and my disabilities prevented me fulfilling this dear duty myself, I should be pitied for my misfortune rather than reproached with a crime. I owe my children a living; I secured one for them that was better, or at least more reliable, than any I myself could have provided: This is the primary point to be considered. After this comes the identification of their mother, who must not be dishonoured. 'You know my situation: I earn my living, with some difficulty, from one day to the next. How could I, in

* *Jean-Jacques Rousseau*, II, ix–xx Trans. by John and Doreen Weightman, London (Routledge & Kegan Paul) 1966.

addition, feed a family? And if I were obliged to resort to the writer's craft, how would I achieve the tranquillity of mind necessary for lucrative work, if my garret were filled with domestic cares and the disturbance of children? Writings dictated by hunger bring in little, and this source of income is quickly exhausted. It would therefore be necessary to find protectors and to indulge in intrigue and manoeuvring; to seek some base employment and eke it out by the usual means to make sure that it provided me with a living and was not taken from me; in short, to stoop to all those infamous acts which inspire me with so justifiable a horror. Would I nourish my children and their mother on the life-blood of the needy? Never, Madame. It is better that they should be orphans than that they should have a rascal as their father.

'Afflicted, as I am, with a painful and mortal illness, I cannot hope to live much longer; even if, during my lifetime, I could support these unfortunates doomed to eventual suffering, they would pay dear for the advantage of having been brought up in slightly more refined circumstances than those in which they are at present. Their mother, victimized by my intemperate zeal and burdened with her own shame and her own needs, almost as much an invalid as I am and still less in a position to ensure their upkeep, would be forced to leave them to their own devices, in which case I see no choice for them but to become shoe-blacks or bandits, the first possibility leading very quickly to the second. If, at least, they had been born in wedlock, they would have found it easier to make their way. What would become of them if, at one and the same time, they had to bear the disgrace of their birth and of their poverty?'*

This 'base, ignoble letter', as Guéhenno calls it, must be quoted in full, because here if anywhere the whole disingenuousness of Rousseau's 'sincerity' is betrayed. The man who would be sincere is unconsciously insincere. This confirms the supposition I began with—that a contradiction exists between self-consciousness and sincerity. To be conscious of a self, vis-à-vis other selves, is already to expose that self to corruption. It is not possible to separate the

* *Ibid.*, Vol. I, pp. 257–9. Letter of 20th April 1751, to Mme. Francueil.

self from others without creating a false entity. I do not wish to get involved in Sartre's distinction between a For-itself and an In-itself, but there are many subtle distinctions of this kind to be made, and they all relate to the degree and kind of our consciousness. In particular, 'so long as we considered the for-itself in isolation, we were able to maintain that the unreflective consciousness can not be inhabited by a self; the self was given in the form of an object and only for the reflective consciousness. But here the self comes to haunt the unreflective consciousness. Now the unreflective consciousness is a consciousness of the world. Therefore for the unreflective consciousness the self exists on the level of objects in the world; this role which devolved only on the reflective consciousness —the making-present of the self—belongs now to the unreflective consciousness. Only the reflective consciousness has the self directly for an object.'*

There is the dilemma which haunted Rousseau all his life: there is the inescapable ambiguity of any pretence of sincerity. Only the self not yet present to the reflective consciousness is sincere. The self present in reflective consciousness is a construct of our intelligence, an ego-ideal; and what is ideal is not real. The only reality is Being, non-conscious Being (*être-en-soi*). Being-for-itself and Being-for-others are both, from this strict point of view, degrees of insincerity.

(v)

Sincerity is often confused with spontaneity—by D. H. Lawrence, for example. But spontaneity (and the 'automatism' of the Surrealists) is a physical reflex rather than a state of mind. What Lawrence calls 'the pulsating, carnal self' has nothing to do with the self of Kierkegaard or Sartre, or with the 'moi seul' of Rousseau. Lawrence was not so much concerned with the Self as a separate entity: rather,

* *Being and Nothingness*. Trans. Hazel E. Barnes, London. 1957, p. 260. Cf. also Martin Buber's discussion of the Self in *Between Man and Man*. Trans. R. G. Smith, London (Routledge & Kegan Paul) 1947, *passim*.

he would deny the possibility (or desirability) of such separateness. 'Give me nothing fixed, set, static. Don't give me the infinite or the eternal: nothing of infinity, nothing of eternity. Give me the still, white seething, the incandescence and the coldness of the incarnate moment: the moment, the quick of all change and haste and opposition: the moment, the immediate present, the Now.'*

Such an identification of the self with the Moment, the quick of Time, is really a losing of the self, a dissolution of the self in animal sensation. If we are to identify such carnality with sincerity, sincerity loses all moral value. Whether it loses all aesthetic value is another question: the question, already referred to, of expressionism. Art, in my opinion (and in the opinion of Valéry, Eliot, Yeats and Proust) is precisely the search for the infinite and the eternal. If the self is by definition fluid, inconsistent, incandescent, it follows that the self can never be a fit subject for a work of art. The more spontaneous (and in this sense sincere) the expression of the pulsating, carnal self, the less aesthetic (artistic). The dilemma seems to be inescapable.

As for automatism, it substitutes for the pulsating, carnal self the promptings of the unconscious. There are degrees of unconsciousness—degrees of depth and degrees of organization. There is no doubt that some dreams have form in the sense of dramatic form: one cannot exclude the hypothesis of 'unconscious' form, that is to say, of forms elaborated in the mind without the conscious participation of the individual (this altogether apart from Jung's hypothesis of 'archetypal forms'). The projection of such forms serves to distinguish surrealism from expressionism. Surrealist poetry and painting are not always automatic in any mechanical sense. The images are arranged and even modified in the act of recording them (if only by the process of *Gestaltung*: perceptual coherence, etc.). The images in the poetry of Eluard or in the paintings of Max Ernst are effectively organized. They may rise automatically to the surface of consciousness, but they then assume a functional coherence (the 'composition' of the poem or painting).

* *Phoenix*. London, (Heinemann) 1936, p. 219.

If the form of the dream is unconscious in origin, it remains inaccessible as a work of art. R. G. Collingwood made this distinction: 'It (the dream) is essentially a structure which is, in the terminology of the psychoanalyst, *unconscious*. The dreamer himself is unaware of it until, in collaboration with his psycho-analyst, he brings it to light. The mythological way of stating this fact is to say that the structure was "in the unconscious". This is frankly nonsense . . . because the structure is not in the unconscious but precisely in the dream, for it is the structure of the dream; and the dream is conscious enough . . . the revelation made by psycho-analysis is not the bringing into consciousness of what was unconscious, but the bringing into explicitness of what was implicit, the noticing of something already actually experienced in a light in which it had not been noticed before . . . the new light in question is nothing but the hitherto overlooked structure of the experience in question . . .' The unconscious, in Collingwood's opinion, is 'a false abstraction'. The reality is 'the implicit logical or structural element in the dream'. The dreamer is unaware of this structure—that is to say, the structure belongs to the dream and can only be separated from it by a false abstraction.*

This may strike the reader as an unnecessarily subtle distinction, but it is fundamental to our problem of sincerity. What becomes of Lawrence's 'pulsating, carnal self' if even his dreams are subject to organization, an organization that he does not control, 'thought in the form of intuition'. Collingwood's point is that the dreamer does not know that he is an artist. The dream must be made explicit, and in so far as the dreamer becomes an artist, 'his artistic creation is a self-critical creation, and the criticising moment or concept—the idea of structure or relevance—is always in advance of the criticized moment, the flow of imaginations which it controls'. Gone, therefore, is any question of spontaneity, and of sincerity.

Collingwood defines art as a concrete or sensuous activity (at the same time 'a life of discipline and endeavour, a struggle to realize

* Quotations from *Speculum Mentis or The Map of Knowledge*. Oxford (Clarendon Press) 1924, pp. 92–4.

one's being in this way and not in that') and sensuous means 'intuitive, immediate, *innocent of explicit reason*'. But the snag in this definition is the word 'explicit', for like all Croceans Collingwood believed in a form of reason that is not explicit, but intuitive. And intuition is associated with innocence, and therefore (by implication) with sincerity. But the innocence of art (its 'absence of social or historical structure') 'is, in point of fact, tempered by the existence, even in art, of implicit thought; but this implicit thought . . . remains hidden from the artist as such.' (*op. cit.*, p. 191.) So what is conceded with one hand (i.e., innocence) is taken away with the other (i.e. the artifice implied by the word 'thought').

The spontaneous is never without form; art is never wholly spontaneous. What remains that is substantial of the concept of sincerity?

(vi)

'Philosophical anthropology is not intent on reducing philosophical problems to human existence and establishing the philosophical disciplines so to speak from below instead of from above. It is solely intent on knowing man himself. This sets it a task that is absolutely different from all other tasks of thought. For in philosophical anthropology man himself is given to man in the most precise sense as a subject. Here, where the subject is man in his wholeness, the investigator cannot content himself, as in anthropology as an individual science, with considering man as another part of nature and with ignoring the fact that he, the investigator, is himself a man and experiences his humanity in his inner experience in a way that he simply cannot experience any part of nature—not only in a quite different perspective but also in a quite different dimension of being, in a dimension in which he experiences only this one part of all the parts of nature. Philosophical knowledge of man is essentially man's self-reflection (*Selbstbesinnung*), and man can reflect about himself only when the cognizing person, that is, the philosopher pursuing anthropology, first of all reflects about himself as a person. The principle of individuation, the fundamental fact of the infinite variety of human persons, of whom this one is only one person, of this constitution and no other, does not relativize anthropological knowledge; on the contrary, it gives it its kernel and its skeleton. In order to become genuine philosophical anthropology, everything that is discovered about historical and modern man, about men and women, Indians and Chinese, tramps and emperors, the weak-minded and the genius, must be built up and crystallized round what the philosopher discovers by reflecting about himself. That is a quite different matter from what, say, the psychologist undertakes when he completes and clarifies by reference to his own self in self-observation, self-analysis and experiment, what he knows from literature and observation. For with him it is a matter of individual, objectivized processes and phenomena, of something that is separated from connexion with the whole real person. But the philosophical anthropologist must stake nothing less than his real wholeness, his concrete self. And more; it is not enough for him to stake his self as an *object* of knowledge. He can know the *wholeness* of the person and through it the wholeness of *man* only when he does not leave his *subjectivity* out and does not remain an untouched observer. He must enter, completely, and in reality, into the act of self-reflection, in order to become aware of human wholeness. In other words, he must carry out this act of entry into that unique dimension as an act of his *life*, without any prepared philosophical security; that is, he must expose himself to all that can meet you when you are really living. Here you do not attain to knowledge by remaining on the shore and watching the foaming waves, you must make the venture and cast yourself in, you must swim, alert and with all your force, even if a moment comes when you think you are losing consciousness; in this way, and in no other, do you reach anthropological insight. So long as you "have" yourself, have yourself as an object, your experience of man is only as of a thing among things, the wholeness which is to be grasped is not yet "there"; only when you *are*, and nothing else but that, is the wholeness there, and able to be grasped. You perceive only as much as the reality of the "being there" incidentally yields to you; but you do perceive that, and the nucleus of the crystallization develops itself'.*

(vii)

I leave this quotation from Buber's essay on "What is Man?" in splendid isolation because it is the only conceivable answer to the question I have been posing throughout this essay. To ask 'What is sincerity?' is in effect to ask 'What is man?' What I like about Buber's 'principle of individuation' is that it is conceived as an activity. It is not enough to examine the self, to confess, to narrate a past experience. That is to treat yourself as an object, as a thing among things. You only become aware of the reality of the self when that self is involved in the business of life, with 'the unbroken wholeness of events, and especially with the unbroken natural connexion between feelings and actions'. This may seem to lead us back to Lawrence's carnal self, even to the "Sachlichkeit" of Stirner's 'Unique One'. But this is not Buber's meaning, for 'in the moment of life he has nothing else in his mind but just to live what is to be lived, he is there with his whole being, undivided, and for that very reason there grows in his thought and recollection the knowledge of human wholeness'. (*op. cit.*, p. 157.)

Wholeness (the achievement of a process of individuation, as described by Buber and Jung) is finally the concept that must replace the ambiguous notion of sincerity. Later in this volume† I shall give some account of the *process* as described by these two great contemporaries, one who liked to call himself an anthropological philosopher, the other who liked to call himself a scientific psychologist; both being above all great humanists. I knew and respected both men: they were the most persistent influences in the latter part of my own life. They were both immensely impressive men—physically so, in that they confronted me as multidimensional

---

* Martin Buber. *Op. cit.*, pp. 123–5. Fontana Edition (Collins), pp. 154–6.

† See pages 73-4, 86-91 and 122-140 below.

'presences'. Their learning was immense, but it was not an elaborate façade, all darkness within. They held their great knowledge in luminous suspension, and each in his own way had achieved the knowledge of human wholeness. It was difficult for them to convey this knowledge in an age committed to the superficial media of mass communication, to a world distracted by war and political hysteria. Those who came into direct contact with them were many, but few in terms of the millions of alienated and fragmented inhabitants of our world. There have been other great men in our time, but these two, and the poet to whom I have devoted a separate 'memoir', are the greatest of whom I can speak as in some sort a humble disciple.

(viii)

I seem to avoid the final issue—perhaps have done so all my life. Buber believed in a personal relationship with 'the spirit of God', 'the image of God', whom he also called 'the Creator'. Man is completed, made whole, by exposure to 'the creative Spirit'. Jung was more ambiguous, but when asked whether he believed in God, answered, 'I do not believe: I know'. He knew, not so much from his own experience (as in Buber's case) but from his awareness of the spirit of God in other people, the people who came to him for healing, and whom he could not heal without God's help.

I cannot bear witness to the presence of God either in Buber's sense or in Jung's sense, and yet I am not a materialist. All my life I have found more sustenance in the work of those who bear witness to the reality of a living God than in the work of those who deny God—at least, the witness of the deniers, Stirner, Marx, Nietzsche, Freud, Shaw, Russell has been out-balanced by the witness of those who affirm God's existence—George Herbert, Pascal, Traherne, Spinoza, Kierkegaard, Hopkins, Simone Weil. In that state of suspense, 'waiting on God', I still live and shall probably die. I have felt no inclination to dramatize this conflict as some 'dark night of the soul', and the resolutions of it that I have expressed in such poems as "The Gold Disc" and "Moon's Farm" are stoical rather

34

than defiant. Maybe I have not suffered enough, or been sufficiently conscious of the suffering of others, to need the kind of consolation that a saint such as Simone Weil found in God. Behind every 'sincere' belief I detect a special kind of experience which has not come to me. Simone's is particularly moving to me:

'In 1938 I spent ten days at Solesmes . . . There was a young English Catholic there from whom I gained my first idea of the supernatural power of the Sacraments because of the truly angelic radiance with which he seemed to be clothed after going to communion. Chance—for I always prefer saying Chance rather than Providence—made of him a messenger to me. For he told me of the existence of those English poets of the XVIIth century who are named metaphysical. In reading them later on, I discovered the poem of which I read you what is unfortunately a very inadequate translation. It is called *Love*. I learnt it by heart. Often, at the culminating point of a violent headache, I make myself say it over, concentrating all my attention upon it and clinging with all my soul to the tenderness it enshrines. I used to think I was merely reciting it as a beautiful poem, but without my knowing it the recitation had the virtue of a prayer. It was during one of these recitations that, as I told you, Christ himself came down and took possession of me.'*

* From a letter to Father Perrin. *Waiting on God*. Trans. by Emma Craufurd. London (Routledge & Kegan Paul) 1951 pp. 20–1. To save the reader the trouble of referring to another volume, I give the text of Herbert's poem:

> Love bade me welcome: yet my soul drew back,
>   Guiltie of dust and sinne.
> But quick-ey'd Love, observing me grow slack
>   From my first entrance in,
> Drew nearer to me, sweetly questioning,
>   If I lack'd any thing.
>
> A guest, I answer'd, worthy to be here:
>   Love said, You shall be he.
> I the unkinde, ungratefull? Ah my deare,
>   I cannot look on thee.
> Love took my hand, and smiling did reply,
>   Who made the eyes but I?

Herbert's poem is well known to me too, though I do not know it by heart; I have read it many times and might read it many more without its having any effect of this kind on me. A long period of preparation had preceded Simone Weil's reading of the poem: she was charged with some mental energy (the violent headaches are significant) which the poem 'touched off'. It need not necessarily have the same effect on a single other person. To those who have not received it, the grace of God seems to be an arbitrary gift, and I resent the suggestion of the initiates that we who live in outer darkness do so because of our intellectual pride. I am completely humble in my attitude to the mystery of life, and accept gratefully such intuitions as come to me from the writings of the mystics, and from works of art. Simone says that one of the principal truths of Christianity, 'a truth which goes almost unrecognized today, is that the looking is what saves us'. I look everywhere, but I do not find. Especially have I looked in the realms of poetry and art. Simone says that 'the soul's natural inclination to love beauty is the trap God most frequently uses in order to win it and open to it the breath from on high'. This may be true, but I have not been caught. I do not believe that the breath comes from 'on high', but rather from below. The *Ta Hsüeh* (Great Learning), the Chinese classic that is the repository of the world's most ancient wisdom, says:

'The men of old who wished to exemplify illustrious virtue throughout the world, first ordered well their own states. Wishing to order well their states, they first had to make an ordered harmony in their own families. Wishing to do this, they first had to cultivate their individual selves. Wishing to do this, they first rectified their minds. Wishing to do this, they first had to seek for absolute sincerity in their thoughts. Wishing for absolute sincerity in their thoughts, they first had to extend their knowledge to the utmost.

Truth Lord, but I have marr'd them: let my shame
  Go where it doth deserve.
And know you not, sayes Love, who bore the blame?
  My deare, then I will serve.
You must sit down, sayes Love, and taste my meat:
  So I did sit and eat.

Such extension of knowledge lies in the investigation of things.'

That chain of being is absolute and there is no other way of achieving a knowledge of good and evil. But there is no question here of a knowledge of good and evil and I do not believe it is ever possible to separate good and evil in the individual self. Good and evil are in some cases (the anthropological sense) interdependent (as are love and hate) and we remain, in spite of all our endeavours (in spite of even the grace of God) in a permanent state of ambiguity, of openness to experience. That state of openness is the only meaning I can give to sincerity in my thoughts. A final or fixed state of goodness would be lifeless—as mortal as a fixed and final state of evil. I may become aware of the evil part of my thoughts by 'the investigation of things' (including the investigation of the behaviour of others), for then I become aware of a lack of harmony in the family and in the state. But at the same time and by the same means I become aware of the good part of my thoughts and of the harmony that can be achieved by the family and the state.

This may seem like a simple pragmatic doctrine to substitute for all the subtleties of Kierkegaard, Buber and Simone Weil. Such as it is, it harmonizes all the thoughts I have ever had on these moral and spiritual problems. I will prevaricate no longer . . .

II

The Truth of a Few Simple Ideas

In the heart of London, just to the north of Trafalgar Square, there is a statue of an almost forgotten heroine of the First World War, Edith Cavell, and on the pediment are inscribed the words: *Patriotism is not enough.* I have been told that these words, which are supposed to have been spoken by Nurse Cavell just before she was executed by the Germans in 1915 for treason, are apocryphal—in any case, like most sayings of the kind, they are ambiguous. What the saying presumably means is that a sentiment such as patriotism is inferior to a love of humanity that does not distinguish between people of one race or another. What is patriotism? Love of one's country and of one's fellow countrymen. But in our time such love has been confused with nationalism, which usually implies hatred of all foreigners and a determination to assert, by force if necessary, the selfish claims of one's own country. Dr Johnson thought that patriotism was the last refuge of a scoundrel, and it is generally considered by moralists that it is more altruistic to proclaim oneself a citizen of the world, to profess the brotherhood of mankind. Such perhaps is the real significance of the words inscribed on Nurse Cavell's monument.

I have learned to distrust all such words, and the lesson began about the same time that Nurse Cavell was sacrificing her life. I very nearly sacrificed my own life in that same war, and for four long years I was asking myself: For what purpose? I was certainly not inspired by any patriotic feelings, or by any feelings of hatred for an enemy. I was caught in the war like a young animal that had sprung some trap, and I stepped into it without the least trace of patriotic sentiment, without enthusiasm of any kind, except a vague desire for adventure, for an ordeal that would test my courage. Those vague desires were quickly dispelled by the crude horrors of the actual experience. I endured these to the end, but long before the end I had lost the adolescent enthusiasm that lent some glamour to the early days of training and embarkation. As the war proceeded and hundreds of thousands of my fellow infantrymen were killed (many of them men I knew and loved) I acquired a deep hatred of those slogans with which the war was being justified by our politicians and journalists. I did not yet have the necessary experience to guard against the substitution of other, equally deceptive slogans —or 'rogue words' as Ruskin called them—and though I hesitated between socialism, communism and anarchism to describe the political ideals I was formulating (the last was the one I eventually adopted), there was one word I did not hesitate to use: pacifism. I continued to fight, for the very good reason that I could not desert my companions, and for the less good reason that I did not wish to be thought a coward, but I did not hesitate to write and publish poems condemning war and expressing a longing for peace.

I have remained a pacifist all my life, and if I am told that pacifism is merely another rogue word, devoid of realism and apt to deceive innocent people, I answer that it represents the essential creed of all the profoundest teachers the world has ever known— Lao-tzu, Confucius, Christ, St Francis, Comenius, Kant, Tolstoy, Gandhi and many others. Pacifism must, of course, be defined, and aggression, which it opposes, must also be recognized and defined. Pacifism is not a negative doctrine: it is the science of diverting aggressive instincts into creative channels. Such a science is now well understood, and scientists such as William James, Freud, Jung and Konrad Lorenz have removed the roguery from the word. Peace is now a realistic alternative to war.

But it has not yet replaced patriotism and other rogue words in the politics of our time. The most thriving of our present slogans in the Western World is the one which H. G. Wells first formulated as 'making the world safe for democracy'. It has immediately countered by a similar slogan—making the world safe for communism—and half-a-century of political chaos has by now surely taught us that both slogans are meaningless. Democracy, just as a political concept, is meaningless for any society larger than a small city or a rural commune. Our so-called democracies in the Western World are oligarchies subject more or less to periodical revision (which never changes their oligarchical structure), and in this they do not differ essentially from the oligarchies that rule the communist world. The people, in any human corporate sense, do not determine any policies outside their backyards. The world is governed by the representatives of industry, finance, technology, and by bureaucracies in the paid service of these powerful groups— governed, not in the interests of the people as a whole, not even of all the people in any one country, and not even nowadays for personal profit, but primarily for the self-satisfying exercise of power.

So much for the ideals I lost through the experience of war. But there were some that I gained from the same experience, apart from a belief in pacifism. I gained—or rather, I was confirmed in—a belief in the essential goodness of man. This may seem to contradict what I have just written about democratic politics, but it is not man, common man, who is engaged in such politics: the common man is exploited by politicians in every country. My belief in the common man arises directly out of my wartime experience. Who were the men I fought with? For the most part miners and agricultural workers from the North of England, with a sprinkling of clerks, teachers and professional men drawn willy-nilly into the vortex of war. To men accustomed to mines and ditches the trenches were perhaps not physically daunting. There were, of course, a few exceptions, men with some in-built neurosis; but the great majority accepted the constant danger and the frequency of death with a willingness for which, for some reason, the French word *insouciance* seems appropriate. It was not that they wished to die, but they knew that death was in any case their human lot—that every bullet, as they used to sing, has its billet. Words such as bravery or courage they would have rejected—they groaned when some visiting general called them 'my brave men'. They were, simply, fatalists, and that is perhaps the philosophy of all men who are engaged in a dangerous calling—miners, sailors, soldiers, airmen, mountaineers. This was the basic characteristic of the men I became familiar with—useful in warfare, but not induced by it. The quality that then emerged among these fatalists I have been inclined in the past to call 'solidarity' (it has nothing to do with the conventional 'esprit de corps'), but recently my attention was drawn to some words of Conrad's (himself a man who had lived dangerously) in the book he called *A Personal Record*:

' . . . Those who read me know my conviction that the world, the temporal world, rests on a few very simple ideas; so simple that they must be as old as the hills. It rests notably among others, on the idea of Fidelity.'

Fidelity is the word I need to describe the simple idea that was revealed to me in the First World War—the fidelity of one man to another, in circumstances of common danger, the fidelity of all men in a group to one another and to the group as a whole. I read, either during the war or shortly afterwards, Kropotkin's great book on *Mutual Aid*, and there I found this simple idea enshrined in a philosophy of society; and to this simple idea I have now been faithful for more than fifty years.

It is a striking paradox that this idea of fidelity, highly valuable as a social bond, is not a moral idea. It came to me in the midst of war, and it characterized groups of men who were, after all, engaged in the beastly business of killing other men. We had sufficient contact with the enemy to know that they too were inspired by the same fidelity to one another; and of course the idea is not confined to men at war—it can characterize any group engaged in a dangerous occupation—even groups of criminals, gangsters as we significantly call them. The lesson here is that social virtues are not necessarily moral virtues: courage, fidelity, self-respect and even love are *social* virtues, and as such are inculcated, not by precept, but by example and habit.

This lesson that I learned so early in life has, I think, been the profoundest of all, and in some sense it determined the rest of my life. But it is by no means the only lesson that I have learned, and it was not, in the usual sense of the phrase, a disillusioning lesson. What was disillusioning was the discovery that an ideal that had proved to be so necessary in war was not viable in peacetime—that fidelity and mutual aid were powerless against the political establishment at home. I have spoken elsewhere (in my autobiography, *The Contrary Experience*) of the intense disillusionment that followed the First World War, a disillusionment shared by ex-combatants in every country (not excluding Russia). This disillusionment has been prolonged for more than half a century, has been intensified by another World War, and is now aggravated by what we call the Cold War. It has found expression in all kinds of movements and revolts, and has provoked noble utterances from such outraged men as Gandhi, Russell and Camus. But what has been achieved? Even the delusive emancipation of India has led only to the martyrdom of Gandhi, to religious and racial strife, to political chaos and famine. The simple idea of fidelity has not prevailed, least of all in India.

I must now speak of the more intimate lessons I have learnt—not in my personal life, for that, apart from the inevitable tragedies of death and separation, has been happy. The severest lessons have been those that have taught me to moderate my personal ambitions. My greatest ambition was to be recognized as a poet, but I soon learned that the modern world has little use for poets in general, and less for me in particular. Against such a statement might be brought in evidence the careers of Yeats, Valéry, Rilke, Frost or Eliot—poets who have been acclaimed and honoured by the whole world. But what do these poets themselves say about their so-called success? They are full of personal bitterness, contempt for society, spiritual disillusionment. They knew that their fame was a hollow and insubstantial show, that their public was largely sycophantic or hypocritical, and that their influence on their fellow-men (compared with the influence of a Dante, a Milton, or a Wordsworth) was as nothing. It is true that their verse was not so 'uplifting' as the verse of the earlier poets I have mentioned; it would have been false if it had been, for the poet today is called upon not to uplift but to reveal —to reveal the tragic situation of modern man. Such a tragic vision is not welcomed by the citizens of an affluent society, and all these poets (not notably 'democratic' in their sentiments) have been ignored by that society. Their reputations are academic, or at best 'aristocratic': they mean nothing to the technocrats who are making the modern world, nor to those who are content to live in such a world.

In my own case I have to confess rather ruefully that I was not born with a tragic view of life—my ideal was to celebrate in poetry, not so much nature, as man's triumph over nature. I remember many discussions with Eliot and other contemporaries of mine on this question of the necessity of a tragic sense of life, and though (under the influence of Nietzsche, Unamuno, Freud and T. E. Hulme) I had come to accept such a necessity *intellectually*, I could not bend my muse in this direction. I attempted one tragic poem of adequate scope ("The End of a War") but even this had to end with an affirmation of hope.

The lesson I learnt from this experience was that as a poet I was not in tune with the age—in spite of the fact that I was a modernist in technique and had never relaxed the intolerable struggle, as Eliot called it, to match words to feelings. It will be said that in my case the feelings were not profound enough: I prefer to believe that they were not fashionable enough. But I do not say this in any spirit of arrogance: merely I affirm once more Conrad's conviction that the world rests on a few simple ideas; and I do not find that the ideas that prevail today are simple enough.

I come now to an experience that may be said to have redirected the course of my life. My interest in the fine arts had been aroused at the same time as my discovery of poetry, and in the intellectual vacuum of the years immediately following the First World War (in England almost a physical vacuum caused by the slaughter of so many young men of my generation) I was drawn into the struggle to establish the new ideals in painting and sculpture—my first art criticism was written already in 1919. The interval between the two wars was a period of intense activity—a new kind of war, the modernists assailing the entrenchments of tradition and authority. Eventually that war was also won, and one learned much from a struggle distinguished by bitterness on one side and arrogance on the other. But such experiences were shared by many others, and do not call for special comment in the present context. The particular and personal experience I have in mind occurred during the Second World War. The British Council was created in 1940 with the purpose—to quote from its Royal Charter of Incorporation—'of promoting a wider knowledge of Our United Kingdom of Great Britain and Northern Ireland and the English language abroad and developing closer cultural relations between Our United Kingdom . . . and other countries'. A Fine Arts Committee was formed to 'project' British art abroad, and in the years that followed it was to prove very effective. But while the war lasted it was impossible to send valuable works of art across the seas, and as an interim measure it was decided to substitute collections of drawings by British children, which could be packed in light parcels and framed when they reached their destination. I was given the task of selecting such drawings and for this purpose visited a number of schools throughout the country. Several exhibitions were sent abroad and I may perhaps mention here an incident which occurred when one such exhibition was shown in Paris. Picasso came one day and spent a long time looking at the pictures. When he had finished he turned to me and said (in French): 'When I was the age of these children I could paint like Raphael. It took me many years to learn how to paint like these children.' The story has often been repeated, generally in a distorted form, but this is the authentic version.

In the course of collecting such drawings I came to a small village in Cambridgeshire and was there shown a drawing by a girl five years old which she herself called "Snake round the World and a Boat". It had been drawn by the child at home (she was the child of working-class parents) and was entirely spontaneous in origin.

The Truth of a Few Simple Ideas

I was deeply moved because what this child had drawn was one of the oldest symbols in the world—a magic circle divided into segments and known as the mandala, the symbol of the self as a psychic unity, a very ancient symbol found in Egypt and the Far East and throughout Europe in the Middle Ages. In Tantric Yoga such a symbol represents the dwelling-place of the gods. But the symbolism of the child's drawing does not end there, for the Snake round the World may be identified with the Uroboros, again an ancient symbol found in Babylon, in India, Egypt and elsewhere throughout the world (among the Navajo Indians, for example). There are many interpretations of this symbol, many of them having to do with time and eternity, but symbols are never meaningful in the rational sense, and of course this child could not attach a meaning to the symbol she had drawn, and was not even aware that it was a symbol. (The boat, she explained, was for crossing the seas.) I, with my more sophisticated knowledge, could recognize the drawing as a symbol that was archetypal and universal. Such knowledge on my part had been acquired largely from my reading of Jung's works, but what had been an interesting hypothesis had suddenly become an observed phenomenon, a proof. This child of five had given me something in the nature of an apocalyptic experience.

This was not the only experience of the kind. Symbols are present in children's drawings everywhere, and at all ages. But on the basis of the material I collected for the British Council during the war I made a close study of the subject which was published in 1943 as *Education through Art*. The more I considered my material the more convinced I became of the basic significance of the child's creative activities for the development of consciousness and for the necessary fusion of sensibility and intellect. In the course of writing my book the theme became more and more polemical. I do not claim to have discovered any truth that was not known to teachers such as Franz Cizek in Austria and Marion Richardson in England, but I added my observations to theirs and put forward an hypothesis that was nothing less than a new system of pedagogy.

The Truth of a Few Simple Ideas

My point of view was accepted by many teachers, at first in England and then throughout the world. A Society for Education through Art was established in the United Kingdom, and in 1951 an International Society for Education through Art which was sponsored by UNESCO and held its first General Assembly in Paris in 1954. INSEA, as it is called, now has branches throughout the world, but this does not mean that its claim (that art should be made the basis of education) has been widely recognized. It conflicts too directly with the technologically motivated education of advanced industrial societies. But the progress of this 'simple idea' in twenty years has been amazing, and I believe that it may yet conquer the world.

It *may*—I do not express any confidence, for mankind seems to drift towards self-destruction in blind disregard of all that its wise men have said or can say. What indeed is there left to say? We need not go back to the wisdom of the East, to the sermons of Buddha and Christ, the Simple Way of Lao-tzu or the Analects of Confucius; to the wisdom of the Fathers of the Church or of the philosophers of the Enlightenment. We have our own prophets who have spoken in clear voices—Tolstoy, Gandhi, Schweitzer, Freud, Jung, Buber. We know what we should do, but we do not do it. We prefer to remain not so much in an outer darkness, for the lights of wisdom blaze round us; but in a bemused euphoria of a material 'progress' that offers mankind a high standard of living in exchange for his spiritual freedom.

The greatest single deception in my life, as in the life of many idealists, has been the failure of socialism, in which term I include communism. This failure springs from one error and one only, 'the most fatal error', as Shelley called it, 'that ever happened in the world—the separation of political and ethical science'. Tolstoy placed Shelley's statement as an epigraph to one of his latest writings, "An Appeal to Social Reformers" (first published in 1900). Tolstoy recognized that the pursuit of power, whether by the individual or the state, was the root of all the evil we endure, and against power only a spiritual weapon could prevail. 'This spiritual weapon is simply the one known long ago to men, which has always destroyed power and always given to those who used it complete and inalienable freedom. This weapon is but this, a devout understanding of life, according to which man regards his earthly existence as only a fragmentary manifestation of the complete life, and connecting his life with infinite life, and recognizing his highest welfare in the fulfilment of the laws of this infinite life, regards the fulfilment of these laws as more binding upon himself than the following of any human laws whatsoever.' Only such a *religious* conception, Tolstoy concluded, could truly destroy power.

But is this a religious conception? Nicolas Berdyaev, a sympathetic but severe critic of Tolstoy, thought not. 'The Good for him was God. This shows his greatness, but also his limitations.' For Berdyaev something more is necessary—an awareness of 'the significance of the irrational processes of life that permeate us, get hold of us, imperil us, and thereby transcend our rational and moral aims and ends . . . True, no one perhaps had experienced the horror of evil, particularly when it parades in the guise of the Good, with such intensity as Tolstoy, but he remained blind to the dark, irrational, metaphysical source of evil.' That, too, was Jung's opinion, not of Tolstoy particularly, but of all social reformers who think that the world can be changed by rational means.

And so we come to the spiritual void that opens in my own path. I have read Berdyaev and many other Christian apologists, and have been moved especially by two of them, Kierkegaard and Simone Weil. Above all by Simone Weil, the greatest spiritual writer of our time, far profounder in my opinion than Teilhard de Chardin or even Martin Buber. The difficulty I experience with all such Christian apologists is that they rely, for their final argument, on the necessity of grace. They admit that this state of mind is an arbitrary phenomenon—'Grace fills empty spaces but it can only enter where there is a void to receive it, and it is grace itself that makes this void' (Simone Weil). It is not even a simple chance: the odds against the unbeliever are doubled.

In desperation we have recourse to the science of the self, to individual psychology, which teaches us surely enough that reason alone no longer suffices. In particular, reason cannot deal with the problem of evil (consider the miserable failure of our present educational and reformatory measures against crime), nor can it deal with force (which is not necessarily always an ally of evil). In despair of reason we now substitute fear—fear of organized crime, fear of nuclear war—if only we are fearful enough, we assume, we can control such evil forces. But fear is not even a positive instinct—it is the inhibition of all instincts, good as well as bad, a paralysis of the mind. What we need is the peace of mind that comes with self-knowledge, and self-knowledge implies the knowledge of the unconscious processes that cause fear and agression, envy and crime. This self-knowledge may in rare cases come from inner illumination, and happy are those who are vouchsafed it. For mankind at large it must come from what we must call education, ambiguous as the word is—an education that takes into account above all of the symbolic needs of the unconscious—therefore, an education through art. The ideal to be achieved might be called *serenity*—the condition of mind, Buber once said to me, that I seek everywhere and find only in England. I fear he was confusing serenity with our famous *sang-froid!*

Education is perhaps a poor and misunderstood process on which to rely for the salvation of mankind, but I know of no other. If we remember its literal meaning, then it does imply bringing to consciousness what is undeveloped, unrecognized, misunderstood or despised. We must become whole men, and we cannot become whole so long as we leave the foundations of the psyche on tremulous ground. I agree with Jung that the process of education (which he called the process of individuation) may lead the individual back to God—or, as he would have said, bring God back to the individual. But these are questions for the future, and largely questions of nomenclature. The present and urgent necessity is to admit the sickness of man's soul and take practical measures to cure it. I would emphasize the word practical, and even substitute for it the word pragmatic, for it is no longer a question of moral exhortation or of religious revivalism; it is a question of having faith in a few simple ideas, for only such simple ideas have the power to transform the world.

III

What is There Left to Say?

It may be that some people like to indulge in a 'what-might-have-been' about themselves or their careers, but though I admit the possible interest of such an exercise if one may assume an interest in what the writer has actually become, it is in my case a demand for self-examination which I undertake with a suspicion that it is not likely to be either honest or objective. This is a general problem examined in the essay on "The Cult of Sincerity". It is only human to suppose that we have been moulded by circumstances beyond our control; and in every age the circumstances are thought to be peculiarly unpropitious. Nevertheless I begin with the supposition that no other span of half a century in our history can offer quite such an unremitting interference with normal development as that which includes the two world wars experienced by men of my generation. It is not only the direct impact of such wars, but also all they involve by way of regimentation and taxation. Taxation, in particular, I see as the main cause of our growing pains. Since the age of twenty-five I seem to have been expending my main energies in a vain effort to catch up with the mounting demands of the State; and what has been a personal misery for the individual has been a disaster for our joint efforts in the arts. Has any other civilization collected income tax on the earnings of its poets? How much surtax did Shakespeare pay?

The State, no doubt, is my scapegoat for a sense of frustration; and a very seductive goat it can be, offering security, responsibility, honours. That is the first mistake one makes: to compromise with authority. But the kind of gesture that a Rousseau or a Thoreau could make is no longer possible—for the simple reason that a modern state 'liquidates' its Rousseaus and Thoreaus. Thoreau would be imprisoned as a vagrant and tax-evader; Rousseau, who was sufficiently persecuted by the society of his own time, would have nowhere to seek a refuge—he would probably be sent, as Ezra Pound was sent, to a state institution for mental defectives. Even if the writer has money, or can make money by writing best-sellers, it is a vain illusion to think that there is any escape from our predicament. Every writer who retires to an Aegean island, or the Californian desert, or even to nearer and relatively tax-free countries like Switzerland, thereafter undergoes a subtle process of degeneration. It is not necessarily a physical degeneration: it has little to do with climate or *dolce far niente*. It is the workings of a remorse for the desertion of the front line in the cultural battle, a battle that must be waged in the thick of our fragmented and alienated societies. Our poetic virtues must lie, if anywhere, in 'the interpretation of the time,' and to interpret the time we must be part of it.

If stoical endurance (with 'beat' undertones) must be our choice, we cannot be sentimental about the consequences. The arts fight a losing battle in our technological civilization, and I see no hope for them. The poet especially has become an anachronism. He does not possess even the entertainment value of a clown. His verse is read by a diminishing number of fellow-poets, and the Arts Council and the BBC present him with a few leaves of artificial laurel. Solemnly to entertain the idea of a poetic career is an absurdity. Let us dismiss it.

What is there left to say? The only fair question is whether, in these circumstances, the poet is allowed to develop the potentialities of his nature. 'Allowed' is, of course, a question-begging word, but this is a question-begging essay. I was not 'allowed' any of the privileges to which my nature might have entitled me. I was, I believe, lucky in my birthplace, and the first ten years of my life were blissfully happy. Then came the first of those cataclysmic events that disturb the normal course of development: the death of my father, the sudden transition to traumatic experiences in a boarding-school for orphans, the slow climb through parental deprivation and adolescent poverty to the precarious ledge of a provincial university. Then the second cataclysm, the First World War in which I was immediately involved.

All this I have described in *The Contrary Experience* and I do not wish to indulge in any kind of self-pity. But one possibility should perhaps enter into these speculations. At Leeds I studied economics under Arthur Greenwood, and vague political ambitions were stirring within me. Through Greenwood I might have been drawn into the Labour Movement. A political career is a conceivable might-have-been, but my poetic sensibility had drawn me, not to the Labour Party, but to Guild Socialism. I found William Morris and Kropotkin more inspiring than Keir Hardie and Ramsay Macdonald. But even Guild Socialism might have been a career. At the end of the summer term of 1914 a possible future was beginning to take shape. In another year I would have taken my degree; then I would have made my way to London to write for the *New Age* (Orage, its editor, came from Leeds and I already knew several of his friends) and for *The Guildsman*, the periodical founded by G. D. H. Cole. These periodicals did not pay their contributors, but in other ways I would have made a living compatible with these political ambitions.

I should perhaps explain why I was drawn to Kropotkin and Guild Socialism rather than to Marx and Communism. I read *Capital* in 1914 and many other writings of the same tendency. I was never anti-Marxist in the sense of rejecting the theory of surplus-value or dialectical materialism in general; but I could not cast off my agrarian heritage, and Marxism always seemed to me to be a political philosophy for the industrial proletariat. Morris and Kropotkin, by contrast, were on the side of the agricultural worker and the craftsmen, and attributed most of our social evils to mechanization. By every instinct and reason I was on their side of this great historical argument. Useless, therefore, to contemplate an alternative career as a communist politician. It is only when I see communism swayed by a peasantry, as it is to-day in Jugoslavia and China, that my sympathies are engaged.

To continue for a moment with this might-have-been, let us assume that I had successfully graduated in the summer of 1915. Let us suppose I had then decided to seek my fortune in London, and had made contact with Orage. He would have received me and helped me, as he did later on, and I might quickly have found a footing as a literary journalist. But then a void immediately presents itself. Orage would already have been in touch with Ouspensky; for some time he had been absorbed in theosophy and the *Bhagavad Gita*; as editor of the *New Age* he would have met Gurdjieff and Major Douglas. So that imaginary career leads inevitably in a direction I could not have followed (after the war Orage was to ask me to become a disciple of Ouspensky, but after a trial-run of a dozen lectures I turned away). As for Cole, he evidently was bent on an academic career, and though he never wholly renounced the principles of Guild Socialism, he had a conception of realism that after the war allowed him to compromise with a very different kind of socialism or with no socialism at all. I imagine that but for the war the Guild Socialist movement would have grown: I don't for a moment suppose that it would have provided me with a career. But there would have been a beginning, for me as for Richard Aldington or F. S. Flint or any young and impoverished intellectual of the time. It would have been a good moment to be alive. Difficult as it is to recapture after all these years, there was a ferment even in England in those pre-war years—the ferment out of which sprang such strange growths as Ezra Pound's *Cantos* and T. S. Eliot's *The Waste Land*, Joyce's *Ulysses*, and Lawrence's *Sons and Lovers*. The war did not cause this ferment: it almost washed it away.

I believe that this would have been a better because a more normal development: that I should have been poorer for longer, and perhaps have suffered more. There would have been more competition: not T. E. Hulme alone, but many bright young rivals who perished in that desolating war. We should have sorted ourselves into groups, as we did with our diminished numbers after the war;

but the grouping would have been different. Incalculable the difference that Hulme's survival would have made; even Rupert Brooke, we may be sure, would have grown up, and the *English Review* under Ford Madox Ford's editorship might have been the focus for our cultural revolution.

Might have been! In one sense the war had changed nothing. Cubism, expressionism, futurism, imagism—all these movements, all aspects of the one revolution of sensibility, had been born before the war and survived it. But in the purely physical sense the war changed everything, firstly because the younger generation was decimated, and the few who survived were spiritually disillusioned. It was difficult to believe that art was of any importance in the world of Clemenceau and Lloyd George, and we had not to wait long before our *semblables* in Russia were fleeing from a tyranny worse than the one they had helped to destroy. We were also changed by the actual experience of war. To come back to my own case, which is the purpose of this essay, I still do not know whether the thing I stepped on in August, 1914, was a snake's head or a ladder. Materially it could be thought of as a ladder, for it gave me four years of material security (under the constant threat of death and the daily presence of suffering). Such an 'ordeal by fire' no doubt gave me also a self-confidence that would have taken longer to acquire in civil life. But at the end it left me with a pathetic longing for security. I have never written about the real horror of fighting, which is not death nor the fear of mutilation, discomfort or filth, but a psychopathic state of hallucination in which the world becomes unreal and you no longer *know* whether your experience is valid—in other words, whether you are any longer sane. In the spring of 1919, demobilized, the spirit of adventure, in any physical sense, was exhausted. One was grateful to recover reality in the shape of the blood-money (war gratuity) given to us on demobilization. With that one could make a new beginning. 'Reconstruction' was the word we were told to repeat. Eliot used to sing a ballad entitled "The Reconstructed Rebel" and that seemed to express our mood of disillusionment. Arthur Greenwood offered me a post

in the Ministry of Labour; I accepted and became a committee-
man. I married and with my gratuity paid the deposit on a little
house in the suburbs. I remember one day telling Osbert Sitwell—
we were crossing Trafalgar Square and I could go to the very spot
to-day—that I was going to be married. He stopped and stood with
a look of great distress on his face, as though I had told him I was
about to commit suicide. He was a little older than I was, and
perhaps wiser. He told me that I was making a serious mistake—
that the poet must remain free, eternally free—that marriage was
economic servitude and spiritual death.

But celibacy also is a spiritual death. We deceive ourselves if we
think we can plan our lives against the grain of our physical dis-
positions. The experience of war left me a fatalist: with Heraclitus
I became convinced that 'war and Zeus are the same thing'—in
other words, that conflict is the ultimate condition of everything, and
particularly this conflict between the disposition of the individual
and the circumstances of his time. My life has been guided by
chance, and that I accept as a natural condition. The people I tend
to dislike are those who have successfully planned their careers:
there is no conflict or contradiction in them because they have
imposed a human ideal (of logic, of purpose, of consistency) on the
divine irresponsibility.

This Heraclitean principle of flux, of chance, of fortuity issues
out of the tragedy of war, and is basic to my anarchism and romanticism. It is a point of view for which only that philosopher of
planning, Karl Mannheim, ever showed any real understanding.
That I can combine anarchism with order, a philosophy of strife
with pacifism, an orderly life with romanticism and revolt in art
and literature—all this is inevitably scandalous to the conventional
philosopher. This principle of flux, the Keatsian notion of 'negative
capability', justifies everything I have done (or not done) in my
life, everything I have written, every attack and defence. I hate all
monolithic systems, all logical categories, all pretences to truth and
inevitability. The sun is new every day.

A fatalistic philosophy should imply more resignation than I have

55

shown. But fatalism does not imply inactivity: on the contrary, since we are counters in a child's game, we are condemned to action. It is in changing, as Heraclitus said, that things find repose. I have called my politics 'the politics of the unpolitical', but I have striven for change, even for revolution. My understanding of the history of culture has convinced me that the ideal society is a point on a receding horizon. We move steadily towards it but can never reach it. Nevertheless we must engage with passion in the immediate strife—such is the nature of things and if defeat is inevitable (as it is) we are not excused. The only excusable indifference is that of Zeus, the divine indifference.

I despair when I think of John Ruskin, for he was a man endowed with sense and sensibility, energy and leisure, who throughout a long life-time fought with eloquence and passionate clarity for the values I have fought for, and in the end was utterly defeated. The younger generations no longer read him and their elders no longer teach them to read him. His numerous works are the cheapest remnants in the boxes reserved for books that nobody will even steal. Yet what Ruskin has to say, about civilization and culture, about art and literature, about politics and economics, is still relevant to the problems of our own time. The evils and wrongs he denounced have continued to flourish since he died more than sixty years ago, a sad and demented old man.

Does it therefore serve any purpose, I have often said to myself (and others have said to me) to fight the same battle with my inferior weapons and without Ruskin's security and leisure? Such questions are never answered, for the reason I have given: there is no rational issue to our strife. I know I have wasted my energies in this vain and bitter struggle, only to see the black claws of an industrial civilization spread over whatever beauty was left in England when Ruskin died. I know it is absurd to oppose the overwhelming forces of technology, usury, philistinism, all aspects of the rationalism that pervades every aspect of modern civilization. But though this is the common-sense and condemnatory view of my life, I know that it could not have been otherwise, and that the battle

which Ruskin engaged must be continually renewed—or we retreat
into despair, silence, or some 'Dirt-dump' like *Finnegans Wake*.

To imagine an ideal career, therefore, is to imagine an unreal
civilization in which this career can unfold. We do not live in a
golden age, or even in the silver age of the Augustans: to flatter
ourselves we may call it an age of steel, but it is an age of gas, of
atomization. Creative artists are oppressed by a sense of the
immense futility of their efforts. This is true of even the most
successful of them: indeed, success on the scale of a Picasso is
always accompanied by a corroding cynicism. The talent (for
genius is innocent) of a Faulkner, a Graham Greene, a Salinger, a
Vladimir Nabokov, a Saul Bellow, derives its energy from an
obsessive hatred of the civilization it depicts. This is not less true
of Joyce, Eliot, Brecht, Beckett: they all write out of *ressentiment*
(in Max Scheler's sense of the term). I was born with an innocence
that is abashed by such cynicism, and for this reason alone I must
retire into silence, or into the sacrificial busy-ness of committees.
There is a poem of Yeats's not often quoted that well expresses my
own condition—"The Curse of Cromwell"—in which he imagines
the lovers and dancers of another age 'beaten into clay', 'all neigh-
bourly content and easy talk are gone.'

> But there's no good complaining, for money's
> rant is on
> He that's mounting up must on his neighbour
> mount,
> And we and all the Muses are things of no
> account.

But then the poet realizes there is another knowledge that proves
things both can and cannot be. We can still be the servant of those
ladies and swordsmen; though they are underground they will still
pay us for a verse. He dreams of a great house,

> Its open lighted doorway and its windows all alight,
> And all my friends were there and made me welcome too;

but this is the illusion, the dreams of a ceremony of innocence that has gone for ever; for when Yeats woke he found himself

> . . . in an old ruin that the winds howled through;
> And when I pay attention I must out and walk
> Among the dogs and horses that understand my talk.

As I relate this fable the pattern of my cloud-cuckoo-land becomes clearer. I never met Ralph Hodgson, but I have always respected his name and in my early verse was much influenced by him. He went out and walked among the dogs and horses that understood his talk, and was not heard of for forty years. Someone who visited him on his farm in Ohio shortly before his death told me that his material circumstances were not good, and it seems that the swordsmen and the ladies did not often keep him company, or pay for a verse. But I think his decision was the right one, and now I fancy that if I had my life over again I would return to the dogs and horses that waited on my father and forefathers for uncounted generations. This, of course, will seem a sentimental and evasive solution to the problem of the poet in a fragmented civilization; but I don't intend the alternative in any spirit of escapism. Ralph Hodgson was not a 'gentleman farmer' and I would not want to be one myself. Nor would I want to be the kind of farmer who sits in an office and directs the activities of a group of tractor-drivers. Tractor-drivers would not understand my talk. C. F. Ramuz and Jean Giono in our time have lived natural lives and they too are writers who have written as I would like to have written, and have yet lived in contact not only with peasants and animals, but with other creative spirits—Ramuz collaborated with Stravinsky, for example, and Giono is not an escapist: his work is a challenge to our sophisticated values.

Sooner or later the dogs and the horses will return, as in Edwin Muir's impressive poem; either they will return, restoring the ceremonies of innocence, or the civilization so much admired by Sir Charles Snow will blow itself up or die of dearth. It is not a question of sentimentality or of nostalgia. Life is not mechanic: it is dogs and horses, roots and branches, seeds, seminal fluids, growth and form. It is these things basically, and above these are 'the lovers and the dancers', the celebrants of a culture.

> O what of that, O what of that,
> What is there left to say?

This is the refrain to "The Curse of Cromwell" and it is the conclusion of this meditation on the mind behind the mask.

While meditating I received the latest issue of the *Evergreen Review*, an incongruously-named periodical, for it is as parched and crinkled as the leaf in Eugenio Montale's poem:

> . . . l'incartocciarsi della foglia
> riarsa . . .

But these parched and crinkled leaves are the laurels of the beatniks and the drug-addicts, of the 'pop'-artists and the Californian buddhists, and it is towards a last phase of disintegration that the course of our despairing poets and painters is now set. I see no other path in California, or in Paris or in London. In the people's communes in China I saw poems written by peasants and pinned up on the notice-board in the village hall; no doubt not very good poems, but *millions* of them are written among the pigs and the water-buffaloes and from such a ferment an essence will remain.

IV

Apology for E.S.

I first met the subject of this memoir in April, 1919. On demobilization after the First World War we had both been appointed to administrative posts in the Civil Service, and for a few months we shared a room in Whitehall, overlooking the Horse Guards Parade. In the initiatory period, before we had formed friendships more in accordance with our distinct personalities, we were much thrown together. We had not yet joined one of the Clubs frequented by civil servants, and would often go in search of a cheap and congenial restaurant where we could lunch. I was not destined to stay in the Civil Service—my real ambitions lay elsewhere, in the world of literature. But Eugene Strickland was a born administrator. During the war he had risen rapidly from the ranks and ended as a brigadier-general at an unprecedented early age. It was obvious that he would be given quick promotion in the Civil Service, but those first months of return to civilian life were a period of confusion, of sorting and shuffling, and Eugene Strickland had to wait his turn.

I did not at first succeed in penetrating the reserve of this strange man, but I was talkative and he listened to me with interest. I even once or twice introduced him to the young poets with whom I was forming associations and planning revolutions, but his attitude to them was one of icy disdain. I did succeed in discovering that he too had once had literary ambitions, and I learned from others that at Oxford he had won a poetry prize of some kind. Though the son of an obscure clergyman of the Church of England, the family was one that in the past had included philosophers and theologians of some distinction. All this was chilling to my warm, incautious zeal, but I suppose that there must have been something in my personality which attracted him, and which in due course led to the confession which has prompted this short memoir.

It is characteristic of him that this confession was not made orally. He sent it to me several months after our ways had parted. I had given him a copy of my first volume of poems. I felt obscurely that he had been critical of my lack of ambition in the Civil Service, and I was therefore eager to justify myself in the eyes of someone whom I admired and whose judgement I could respect. I did not ask for his opinion of my work, and I did not expect that he would do more than acknowledge the gift. Instead, quite unexpectedly, it was himself that he felt he had to criticize: he had to defend himself against the charge I was silently making, that he had in some sense betrayed a sacred trust. His apology began in this manner:

'I shall treasure your volume as a memorial of our brief friendship, but you must forgive me if I do not comment on it. In a certain sense that would be too painful for me, for reasons which I shall try to explain to you. I too was born a poet. That is not an arrogant claim for there is a soul of poetry in every child, did we but know how to recognize it and preserve it: a bright ecstasy that fades more or less slowly according to our circumstances. In most cases it disappears altogether during that period of "latency", as the psychologists call it, between the age of eleven and eighteen, when so many of our primitive instincts sink below the level of consciousness. Then at puberty a creative impulse may suddenly revive again. But by then it has to contend with other desires and ambitions. The adolescent mind becomes a ghostly battlefield, on which the victory will go, not to the strongest, but to the one that finds the firmest foothold in conscious life.

'That I was from the moment of my birth destined to be a poet is now a conviction I cannot share with anyone else. I have effectively destroyed all the evidence. In any case it would be more exact to say I was born with a sensibility that was acute (as is the sensibility of all children brought up in a natural environment) but one that was diffuse and wayward. According to the circumstances that then began to determine my development, I became a poet because words were the first tools that were put into my hands to express the desperate need I had to find signs or symbols for my inmost feelings. It seems clear to me now that if in my childhood I had been made familiar with other means of expression—colours that I could manipulate into images or stones that I could carve—I might have become a painter or a sculptor, but living in a remote country parish, the child of unsophisticated parents, I was never made familiar with these arts—I had almost no knowledge of their existence. But words were not only spoken to me, with a clear and musical accent, but were also read to me, as fairy-tale or holy verse. I seized on them from the beginning, as a gift from God, given me to play with and eventually, when I was grown up, to work with.

'Several years were to pass before I discovered that words had a purpose of this kind. The daily usage I made of speech was at first a sufficient art, and it was only when I went to school and was taught that speech had uses other than the communication of feeling that I became aware of some sundering of my very self. From that moment I spoke two languages—the inner language that expressed my feelings and the outer language that I addressed to other people to satisfy their expectations. I answered the questions that tested my knowledge of the world, and discovered, as all children do, that in order to please my parents and teachers, I had to acquire a knowledge of external facts—of numbers, measurements, grammar and history. The language of my feelings I might still use for intimate occasions, to convey to those I loved my affections and desires; but it so happened that my family life came to a sudden end in my tenth year and I was then suddenly thrown into an alien world where there was no use for a language of feeling. My sensitive antennae recoiled into my innermost being, and for eight years I remained a dumb and frightened animal.

'When I went to Oxford in my eighteenth year, I discovered that the repressed language of feeling had another name, and could be spoken again as poetry. This was a revelation that transformed my life, but it was not at first a revelation that could be shared with others: poetry became a secret activity and it was only by accident that one or two sympathetic friends became aware that I was writing verse.

'It was they who encouraged me to take that further and fatal step of showing my poems to strangers—and eventually to submit one of them for a prize.

'I call this a fatal step because I had been taught, by my school-fellows and indeed by everyone I met in the world, that it was manly to hide one's feelings, that language was given to us for that very purpose. But I already knew, from my reading of poetry (which had begun not long before my writing of it) that poetry is not the direct expression of feeling, but is rather the art of inventing forms to contain our feelings, such forms being definite and durable and of interest to other people by reason of their shape and sub-stance rather than their content. The poet has to learn the bitter lesson that his feelings are not unique—indeed, may be quite commonplace. All feelings are amorphous by nature, but interest in others may be aroused if the artist can succeed in giving them significant form. It is the form only that constitutes the objective value of a work of art.

'Then began that difficult and humiliating stage in my life when I was to discover that the shaping of my feelings into objective forms was not a sufficient activity for survival, nor even one that could attract the attention and admiration of the world I lived in. There had been a period, not so remote, when the poet—a few exceptional poets, perhaps—could make a public profession of his activity. Many poets now forgotten lived exclusively as poets and were accepted in that social role. It was soon made evident to me that that was not to be my role, nor the role of any poets in my time. To *expatiate* in verse, to find in verse a public "function", as Milton and Wordsworth had done, this was not possible in a world that no longer listened to poetry as to the voice of wisdom or prophecy.

'It will be seen from this confession that what was taking place in me was a conflict of ambitions. The thought of my own father's brief and obscure life was perhaps always present to my consciousness. No doubt he had been sustained by his Christian humility, and had been very content with his country living. But I had worldly ambitions—not so much for the sake of wealth or social rank, but of power and active participation in public affairs. Already my thoughts were turning to those professions, such as law and politics, which were open to the arts of eloquence. I saw myself addressing vast audiences, swaying their emotions, inducing their loyalty. Then came the war, and you know the rest. My poetic reveries were put away with my civilian clothes; five years later the clothes were moth-eaten and the reveries had vanished.'

The letter ended abruptly, without any regrets or further explanations. I was profoundly moved by Strickland's confession, but not entirely convinced. For many years I was to meditate on his lot, and as I saw him rising higher and higher in the hierarchy of power, it was not possible to refrain from comparing his lot with mine—not that I was ever to envy him, except perhaps in periods of financial stress which are the lot of all writers, but his fame was so much more substantial, his part in public affairs so decisive, that by comparison I felt my own modest achievements to be unimportant, irrelevant to the mighty events through which we had lived. This led me to re-examine the whole basis of my poetic activity, with these present results.

I do not believe that I began with the idea that a poet could have any influence of the kind achieved by a successful politician, civil servant or industrialist. Poetry has perhaps never had that kind of immediate effect: it seeps into the public consciousness and after many years it is recognized that a Dante or a Shelley has formed an intellectual climate in which decisive changes of opinion have taken place. In that sense and only in that sense can we agree with Shelley that poets are the unacknowledged legislators of the world. But that process of absorption and transformation is infinitely subtle and even in the case of poets who have enjoyed great fame, is not easy to trace, except perhaps in the case of those who have been militant patriots, such as Mickiewicz. But these have not been the greatest poets. Major and minor poets there have always been, but the distinction has little to do with the quality of their poetry. Greatness is rather an aspect of energy or character: the ability to sustain the role of poet in a hostile environment. Wordsworth is a major poet, William Blake a minor one; but the poetic quality of their genius cannot be determined in this way—if by poetic genius we mean what Coleridge meant by the word—'originality in intellectual construction: the moral accompaniment, and actuating principle which consists, perhaps, in the carrying on of the freshness and feelings of childhood into the powers of manhood'. Coleridge's definition does imply a sustained effort of some kind (a moral accompaniment to the aesthetic activity), but the essence of it is conveyed in the final clause, which envisages an interpenetration of feeling and form, the feeling being recollected from our first sensations, the form being an original intellectual construction precise enough to recover the innocence and acuity of those first sensations.

To succeed in remembering sensations so remote and so elusive requires a particular kind of effort of such subtlety and strength, that only a determined and consistent attention to the promptings of the mind can ensure success. Such are the sessions of sweet silent thought that Shakespeare evokes; such are the intimations of immortality recollected from childhood by Wordsworth; and such the intermittences of the heart upon which Proust relied for the recovery of his past sensations. The great poets are not in doubt about the source of their creative powers—those 'first affections' and 'shadowy recollections' are 'a fountain light of all our day', 'a master-light of all our seeing'. Once these 'truths' are awakened, neither 'listlessness, nor mad endeavour', can utterly 'abolish or destroy' them.

Listlessness and mad endeavour—Wordsworth uses precise words to indicate the states of mind and body that prevent poetic inspiration. Listlessness implies a lack of moral force, of the ability to concentrate all the mind's faculties on this delicate task of recollection; whereas mad endeavour indicates the much less avoidable distractions demanded by conscious participation in the affairs of the community in which we live.

It is at this point that the choices presented to the young poet become inescapable, and are often insidious in their approach. It is not often that he is aware of their nature; much less often that he is instructed in the fatal consequences of a wrong choice. Only adult hindsight, and some acquaintance with the psychology of inspiration, can bring an understanding of events in themselves spontaneous. Spontaneously the young poet is attracted to certain spheres of knowledge, science or philosophy; spontaneously he acquires friends and falls in love; spontaneously he volunteers for military service or equally spontaneously resists conscription. By a multitude of easy steps he adopts conventional attitudes, and advances into a place made ready for him by his fellow citizens. With each step the shadowy recollections of childhood retreat; their freshness and sensuous charm are lost under the opaque diaphragm we call amnesia.

This is a sufficient explanation of why the period of inspiration in a poet is so short-lived, so difficult to sustain. It is the sufficient explanation of why so few people ever become poets: the clouds of conventional thought and feeling, the 'shades of the prison-house', close upon the growing boy before he has a chance to realize how fugitive are the moments of vision, how little time is given him to polish a mirror to reflect them, to build an 'intellectual construction' to sustain them.

These considerations may or may not have been clearly present in the mind of the young poet we are considering. To listlessness he was never given; on the contrary, he plunged into the challenge of life in the very spirit of mad endeavour, and the more his energies were engaged in this strife, the more conscious he became of their encroachment upon his creative designs. It was at this time, in his twenty-first year and when engulfed in an enterprise he had never for a moment envisaged—namely, war—that he had read and been completely seduced by that 'affectionate exhortation' addressed by Coleridge 'to those who in early life feel themselves disposed to become authors'. The beginning, middle and end of Coleridge's exhortation 'converged to one charge: *never pursue literature as a trade*'. E.S. may not at the time have perceived certain equivocations in the argument that followed. Coleridge himself was a poet, and at the time he wrote this exhortation (1815) was twenty-seven years old, and already woefully conscious of the gradual decline of his own poetic inspiration. He felt he had misused his talents, and in particular that the distractions that now beset him were due to his dependence on his pen for a livelihood. Since poetry did not provide a sufficient income (and could not be 'forced' to do so) he was driven to journalism (*The Watchman, The Friend*), to reviewing, to preaching and lecturing, to *scrounging* for a living by every means open to a man with a ready pen. He then (in his exhortation) conjured up a picture of those scholars and philosophers who had combined an honourable occupation 'with a spare-time literary activity'. 'From the manufactory or counting-house, from the law court, or from having visited your last patient, you return at evening,

> Dear tranquil time, when the sweet sense of home
> is sweetest—

to your family, prepared for its social enjoyments, with the very countenances of your wife and children brightened, and their voice of welcome made doubly welcome by the knowledge that, as far as they are concerned, you have satisfied the demands of the day by "the labour of the day". Then when you retire into your study, in the books on your shelves you revisit so many venerable friends with whom you can converse. Your own spirit scarcely less free from personal anxieties than the great minds that in those books are still living for you! Even your writing desk with its blank paper and all its other implements will appear as a chain of flowers, capable of linking your feelings as well as thoughts to events and characters past or to come, not a chain of iron which binds you down to think of the future and the remote by recalling the claims and feelings of the peremptory present.'

Apology for E.S.

There is a certain truth in all this if *authorship* is all one has in mind, and it is significant that when Coleridge proceeds to give examples of those who have combined 'weighty performance in literature with full and independent employment', not one is a poet as he would define a poet—Cicero and Xenophon, Sir Thomas More, Bacon, Baxter, Erasmus, Darwin and Roscoe. He could not cite his friend Wordsworth, a *dedicated* poet if ever there was one; nor could he cite his myriad-minded Shakespeare, the prototype of all poets. It is true that Coleridge has in mind all the time a profession he had himself all but adopted—that of a clergyman in the established church, and a clergyman in his time could indeed pursue a life of scholarship 'without incongruity'. He could even, in the Bible, find 'the origins or first excitement of all the literature and science we now possess'. Coleridge concludes that it would be 'a sort of irreligion' to question the compatibility of such a profession with the profession of literature. But it is also 'a sort of irreligion' to suppose that the Muse of Poetry is not a jealous muse, or that first affections and shadowy recollections which are the mainspring of poetic inspiration are to be recovered by the routine activities celebrated in Coleridge's affectionate exhortation. Coleridge was deceiving himself; and thereby misleading all those who were to follow his advice in the years to come. But not the object of this memoir, perhaps for the very good reason that his own father had been a clergyman.

The temptations that beset the young poet are of two kinds—social and sentimental. That the poet should withdraw from society altogether and live like a hermit or a monk is perhaps not desirable, because he thereby limits his experience, and tends to retreat into an imaginary world where all is unreal. It is true that in as much as he is a poet he is gifted with a special faculty by means of which he can project his mind into the minds of others, and his senses respond like sympathetic chords to remotest actions and events. But however great his endowment of sympathy, he is nevertheless required to experience the complexity of the human scene, and his own emotions must be educated by such experience. There are degrees, however, of involvement, and as Coleridge himself admitted, the poet always remains a spectator *ab extra*: his emotions may be recollected but his eye is objective: his emotions must 'crystallize' before they can become the substance of a work of art. The Romantic poets, who are so often accused of vagueness and imprecision, are the best witnesses of this necessity. Wordsworth among them perhaps gives the clearest expression of the objective nature of the poet's vision in a short poem whose significance has been ignored:

> Yes! thou art fair, yet be not moved
> To scorn the declaration,
> That sometimes I in thee have loved
> My fancy's own creation.
>
> Imagination needs must stir;
> Dear Maid, this truth believe,
> Minds that have nothing to confer
> Find little to perceive.
>
> Be pleased that nature made thee fit
> To feed my heart's devotion,
> By laws to which all Forms submit
> In sky, air, earth, and ocean.

This little Kantian admonition tells us that all that is fit to afford substance to a poem must conform to certain structural prototypes (or archetypes, as we sometimes call them) that constitute the essential nature of a work of art. A poem is not the spontaneous overflow of emotion (and Wordsworth never said it was); the overflow of emotion is fed into specific and appropriate forms. A knowledge of these forms (which comes from an intuitive understanding of the function of form in the universe) is more important to the poet than any amount of formless emotional experience. Indeed, too much squandering of emotional sympathy may submerge the faculties by means of which we become aware of form, so that the mind, as Wordworth says, having nothing to confer, finds little to perceive.

Apology for E.S.

The young poet, therefore, in the first access of adolescent emotions (not only sexual emotions, but enthusiasms of every kind, religious, political, patriotic) is in great danger of losing sight of the laws to which all poetic expression must submit. This is all the more true if he becomes involved in what one might call the politics of art, expending his energies against lifeless but immovable conventions; but this is nevertheless a struggle that may be forced upon him by the circumstances of his time, as it was forced upon Wordsworth and Coleridge. The situation that E.S. inherited in the first and second decades of the twentieth century, was of this kind. The art of poetry in England had succumbed to conventions that were stultifying because they had ignored the profound changes in sentiment or feeling that had occurred as the inevitable consequence of the social and industrial developments of the nineteenth century —changes that were being prolonged and intensified with every passing year of the new century. Imagination, in such a situation, 'needs must stir'. The young poet is 'called up', to man the literary barricades, to write or distribute manifestoes, to engage all his energies in a revolutionary struggle as fierce as any on the political front. He is necessarily involved—he must help to found a periodical, compose manifestoes, demonstrate his revolutionary zeal in every way open to a writer. But always these polemical activities, mingled and interblended with activities of a more personal kind, weave a knot of greater and greater complexity. Poetry being a jealous Muse is jealous even of those poets who sacrifice their proper energies in her own defence.

To stand aside, perhaps just trimming the traditional sails to these winds of change, is not a possible alternative. Even such a believer in tradition as E.S.'s contemporary, T. S. Eliot, was compelled by the very acuteness of his poetic sensibility to adopt a revolutionary idiom. But to mention this poet is to expose the dilemmas that E.S. refused to face, for the very good reason that he knew he would be defeated. For those who care to look beneath the surface of the 'intolerable stress' that extends from *Prufrock* to the *Four Quartets* there is the tragic spectacle of a poet retreating step by step before the pressures of reason and convention, habit and belief. The confession in "East Coker" is the saddest confession ever made by a poet, and the most fearless:

So here I am, in the middle way, having had twenty years
Twenty years largely wasted, the years of *l'entre deux guerres*
Trying to learn to use words, and every attempt
Is a wholly new start, and a different kind of failure
Because one has only learnt to get the better of words
For the thing one no longer has to say, or the way in which
One is no longer disposed to say it. And so each venture
Is a new beginning, a raid on the inarticulate
With shabby equipment always deteriorating
In the general mess of imprecision of feeling,
Undisciplined squads of emotion. And what there is to conquer
By strength and submission, has already been discovered
Once or twice, or several times, by men whom one cannot hope
To emulate—but there is no competition—
There is only the fight to recover what has been lost
And found and lost again and again: and now, under conditions
That seem unpropitious. But perhaps neither gain nor loss.
For us, there is only the trying. The rest is not our business.

It is dangerous for a poet to admit failure—his enemies are only too willing to believe him. Eliot was a failure of such tragic dimensions that his failure constitutes a new kind of greatness (and therefore of success). The cautious prescience of an E.S. might seem by comparison to be merely the cowardice of the intellectual dandy. But consider this failure for a moment in the light of all those minor poets who still strive so desperately for recognition, like Lilliputians scrambling over the recumbent giant. No race of pygmies is so vicious or so ungenerous. Not content with climbing on the poet who confessed himself defeated (to give themselves an undeserved eminence), they use the heights they thus attain as vantage points for attacking each other. To the vanity of minor artists there is no end, and it is a nice reckoning to judge whether alienated poets, painters or musicians are supreme in spitefulness.

For the modern poet who is determined neither to fight to recover what has been lost (in the manner of E.S.) nor to participate in a pygmy warfare, there is only the patient (and private) endeavour described by Eliot. Such a poet would be well advised, like Eliot's priestly predecessor, not to seek publication during his lifetime; but that is perhaps only to be expected of someone living under a spiritual discipline as strict as that observed by Gerard Manley Hopkins. The free poet (free only in the sense that he is free to dedicate himself wholly to his Muse) is at least not secretive. He may not peddle his wares, but like Cézanne with his paintings, he will allow other people to pick them up and exploit them. And who shall blame a poet if he takes some care to preserve them for a future age, so that what has been lost may be found again, what recovered read under conditions more propitious? It is perhaps a vain hope, but it is all that is left to the modern poet.

Great poets inspire a great and concurrent criticism—and are sometimes great critics themselves. Coleridge is at the head of English critics of poetry, closely followed by Dryden, Pope, Wordsworth, Shelley, Keats and Arnold. In our own age the only creative critics have been considerable poets—Hopkins, Eliot, Stevens. Academic critics have done little but obscure the real nature of poetry, and journalistic critics and impecunious reviewers have at all times written to ease their own afflatus or disguise their own impotence. Though it is questionable whether the critics of verse, of drama, of music or of painting excel in this kind of petulant endeavour, it is the reviewers of poetry who most directly expose themselves, for they will often illustrate their opinions with quotations—which is not so readily done in the other arts. They ask us to admire banal observation or obscure metaphors which fail to support the assertions they have just made. They rarely exhibit a poem as a whole, as a unity, and are so completely ignorant of prosody that they condemn any verse that does not trip along in iambics—or, alternatively, praise lines that are essentially prosaic. Verse of any kind is a pitifully easy target: it can be read in a few minutes and condemned in a few words. Who but the poet himself, or the exceptional few who already possess the volume, can know whether the length of five witty lines in a newspaper is rope enough to hang a poet. But many poets have been strangled at birth by these means.

All these are arguments in support of E.S. He was not a coward, but he was not prepared to submit a partial and intermittent exercise of his talents to the judgement of imperfect critics. He had come to the conclusion early in his life (I suppose in the months immediately succeeding the publication of his prize poem at Oxford) that the age into which he had been born was characterized by a new kind of illiteracy—the illiteracy of those who read but do not reflect, the illiteracy of those for whom words are signs but not symbols. In such a society the poet is as obsolescent as the peasant or the priest. Poetry is not what in the jargon of the age is called a medium of mass communication. That utilitarian function, if it ever belonged to poetry, ceased with the invention of the printed book. All the arts have retreated in the degree that they have been depersonalized by methods of mechanical reproduction and wholesale distribution. Art in reality only exists, in Martin Buber's phrase, 'between man and man', which may explain why a dramatic poet such as Shakespeare (abating the question of his poetic genius) still has a popular appeal, while Spenser, and even Milton, are read exclusively by a cultured élite. The modern poet does not meet an audience face to face, except in arranged poetry readings, which are rare events and too arbitrary and wilful for true dialogue to take place. The necessary relationship between the poet and his auditor, between the I and the Thou, is called 'inclusiveness' by Buber, and he defines it as 'the extension of one's own concreteness, the fulfilment of the actual situation of life, the complete presence of the reality in which one participates. Its elements are, first, a relation, of no matter what kind, between two persons; second, an event experienced by them in common, in which at least one of them actively participates, and, third, the fact that this one person, without forfeiting anything of the felt reality of his activity, at the

73

same time lives through the common event from the standpoint of the other.'* This last is the essential point: the listener must *live through* the common event, which is the poem, from the standpoint of the poet. The modern listener (who is usually a reader) has lost all capacity for this relationship, and it is for this reason, and perhaps for this reason alone, that the true appreciation of poetry is now such a rare experience.

Lacking this mutual relationship with the other one, with an included listener, the modern poet is frustrated, and can only languish in his singularity, his abandonment. Only occasionally will he find another One, a submissive but intelligent listener, such as Hopkins found in Richard Watson Dixon. But this mutual relationship must be multiplied many times before a poet can establish himself—or rather be sure that he has established the unique essence that is his poetic intuition of the experienced reality.

It is difficult for the modern poet to have any confidence in the future of poetry. It is the first art to perish in the depersonalized desert of a cybernetic civilization; music and painting will soon follow, and art in general will cease to be a meaningful dialogue between man and man. What this portends, in terms of humanism and human survival, is not in doubt. The mass civilizations of our time are only viable if the units composing them are uniform. The mechanized state admits no variable components: its only 'ranking order' is a graded efficiency in practical matters; its 'unity' is incompatible with 'individuality' and 'mutuality'. This means the end of art as a human activity, and the gradual atrophy of aesthetic sensibility. The engineers of this new society may invent new forms of communal activity to which they will give the name of art—mass parades, mass ballets, mass concerts. But the enthusiasm generated by such events will not be creative. Rather it will induce in its participants an intoxication which is a *paranoia*, a surrender of the individual mind to a mass emotion—an emotion, moreover, that can be pre-determined for social or political ends. This is not

* *Between Man and Man*. Trans. R. G. Smith, London (Routledge & Kegan Paul) 1947, p. 97.

the way of art. Every work of art is born in the individual consciousness, and finds its fulfilment when it enters the consciousness of
another individual, and creates between these two individuals an
indissoluble bond of mutual understanding and love. There is
nothing *exclusive* in such a relationship: each of any two individuals
can form a mutual bond with a further individual, and in this
manner the web of a natural society is woven. It might be compared
to a chain-mail of interconnected links. But there is a limit beyond
which such links cease to be formed. It is the limit of our love and
understanding of each other and of the natural world we experience
together. As poets we strive to establish ourselves in this mutual
world, and we know that we have succeeded when our words are
received and established in another mind. Thus we construct, cell
by cell, experience by experience, a natural philosophy which
includes 'all Humanity and Divinity together GOD, Angels, Men,
Affections, Habits, Actions, Virtues; every Thing as it is a solid
entire Object singly proposed, being a subject of it, as well as
Material visible Things. But', Traherne wisely qualifies, 'taking it as
it is usually bounded in its Terms, it treateth only of Corporeal
Things, as Heaven, Earth, Air, Water, Fire, the Sun and Stars,
Trees, Herbs, Flowers, Influences, Winds, Fowles, Beasts, Fishes,
Minerals, and Precious Stones; with all other Beings of that Kind'.*
Poetry is this natural philosophy presented from one consciousness
to another, in memorable words.

---

* The Third Century, § 44

V

My Anarchism

> . . . while it is true that the conclusion
> of a syllogism follows from the premisses
> in quite a different sense from that in
> which a knee-jerk follows from the doctor's
> tap, it seems reasonable to say that, just
> as I cannot help jerking my knee, once
> I have been tapped, so I cannot help
> assenting to the conclusion once I have
> grasped the premisses.
>
> D. H. MONRO: *Godwin's Moral Philosophy*

The appearance of a comprehensive collection of writings on the anarchist tradition (*Patterns of Anarchy*, edited by Leonard I. Krimerman and Lewis Perry, New York, Anchor Books, 1966) gives me an opportunity to review my own anarchist convictions, which have now lasted for more than fifty years.—I date my conversion to the reading of a pamphlet by Edward Carpenter with the title *Non-Governmental Society*, which took place in 1911 or 1912, and immediately opened up to me a whole new range of thought—not only the works of professed anarchists such as Kropotkin, Bakunin and Proudhon, but also those of Nietzsche, Ibsen, and Tolstoy which directly or indirectly supported the anarchist philosophy, and those of Marx and Shaw which directly attacked it. I use the word 'conversion' to describe the experience because it was undoubtedly quasi-religious; I was at the same time slipping away from the Christian faith I had acquired from a pious family background. And yet my new beliefs were not idealistic—in spite of all appearances to the contrary, I am not an idealist, but rather, in the sense defined by Unamuno, a quixotist, and a practical rather than a speculative or meditative quixotist. Unamuno tells us that 'the philosophy of Don Quixote cannot strictly be called idealism: he did not fight for ideas. It was of the spiritual order; he fought for the spirit'. In exactly the same way the type of anarchist I am does not fight for ideas: he is not an ideologist of any kind, but rather a pragmatist. The editors of *Patterns of Anarchy* recognize this: 'The positive goal of anarchism, then, can be regarded as a consistently individualized pragmatism.' Philosophically anarchists are nearer to deflaters of idealism such as John Dewey and Karl Popper than to Utopian socialists such as Karl Marx or Lenin. All forms of historicism are profoundly repugnant to the true anarchist.*

Nevertheless, anarchism is a social or political philosophy, and the editors of this anthology, as they proceeded, became 'more and more amazed at how many perceptive social theorists have spoken in the anarchist tradition'. They present fifty-seven selections from forty-one writers, including eight critics of anarchism. There are many other writers they might have quoted, including some who have made important contributions to anarchist thought, such as H. B. Brewster, Gustav Landauer and Martin Buber, and they perhaps rightly exclude those many writers who have expressed an anarchist philosophy though they may never have used the word anarchism—Zeno, Lao Tze, Chuang Tze, Thoreau, Shelley, Nietzsche, Morris, Ibsen, Gandhi, Vinoba, Wilde, Camus, Silone, A. S. Neill and Lewis Mumford. And personally, just for the fun of it, I would have included Marx's famous statement about 'the withering away of the state'.

There is perhaps only one belief on dogma common to all professed anarchists, the fundamental one that is indicated by the

---

* Bakunin made this clear in his criticism of Marx's 'idealism'. The only universal law in human history, said Bakunin, is the struggle for existence. Historicism arises from the fallacy that thought is prior to life, and abstract theory prior to social practice.

word itself in its literal meaning—a way of life *without government*. But this is a negative definition, a fact from which the movement has always suffered, though dialectical philosophers should have recognized that the assertion of a negation always leads to an anti-thesis and a leap forward to some positive doctrine, which in the case of anarchism is the 'consistently individualized pragmatism' mentioned by our anthologists. This positive doctrine requires far more explanation than will be found in *Patterns of Anarchy*, and my present intention is to contribute to such further explanation. But before doing so I would like to mention some legitimate points of difference among anarchists, all of which, however, are resolved in the final synthesis.

The anarchist is committed to the decentralization of power in the political sense; does this also imply decentralization in the economic sense, the reversal of those processes that have led to the big city, the giant factory, the multiple store, and other concentra-tions of human activity? I believe it does, for reasons not essentially anarchist, reasons which are given in one of the contributions to *Patterns of Anarchy*, namely, that such a tendency is 'much more in consonance with the basic trends of modern technics than the centralized State economics of the Marxists . . . Specialization of industry and gigantic units are a liability under conditions demand-ing flexibility and ease of adaption. And they will become super-fluous with the growing mobility of power, its wider distribution from central energy stations'. The writer ("Senex") gives many other reasons which favour this process of decentralization, and in this respect architects such as Frank Lloyd Wright, sociologists such as Lewis Mumford, and contemporary planning experts generally, have come to conclusions similar to those that have always been advocated by anarchists.

But do anarchists accept what is in effect a technological civiliza-tion, or are they, as so many people suspect, instinctive luddites, opposed to the whole concept of mechanization, yearning for a return to a more primitive pattern of life?

There is a certain justification for this suspicion if one confuses

anarchism with the medievalism of Morris and the romantic distri-
butivism of Catholics such as Hilaire Belloc and Chesterton. But
actually most of the leading anarchists have been scientific in their
outlook—Kropotkin, who did so much to establish anarchism as a
political philosophy, notably so. For Kropotkin, as Krimerman and
Perry point out, the justification of anarchism is primarily an
empirical task, 'to be carried out by close and comprehensive
observation of such facts as might be gathered by a biologist or
anthropologist. Human culture manifests an evolving pattern and
direction, which it is the function of the anarchist philosopher to
record, much as celestial motions and patterns are recorded by the
astronomer. And when this is accomplished, so Kropotkin maintains,
it will be clear that anarchist communism is the conclusion towards
which all the data of biology, anthropology, and history are directed.'
As political 'gradualism' this seems to lag behind even the extreme
Fabianism of Karl Popper. Kropotkin's ultimate appeal as a
scientific anarchist, according to Krimerman and Perry, is not
to what ought to be, but to what is or what is steadily evolving. Kropotkin himself renounced all forms of utopianism. The
following extract from one of his little-known pamphlets makes
this clear:

'The anarchist thinker does not resort to metaphysical concep-
tions (like "natural rights", the "duties of the state", and so on) to
establish what are, in his opinion, the best conditions for realizing
the greatest happiness of humanity. He follows, on the contrary,
the course traced by the modern philosophy of evolution . . . He
merely considers society as an aggregation of organisms trying to
find out the best ways of combining the wants of the individual with
those of cooperation for the welfare of the species. He studies
society and tries to discover its *tendencies*, past and present, its
growing needs, intellectual and economic, and in his ideal he merely
points out in which direction evolution goes. He distinguishes
between the real needs and tendencies of human aggregations and
the accidents (want of knowledge, migrations, wars, conquests)
which have prevented these tendencies from being satisfied. And

he concludes that the two most prominent, although often unconscious, tendencies throughout our history have been: first, a tendency towards integrating labour for the production of all riches in
common, so as finally to render it impossible to discriminate the
part of the common production due to the separate individual; and
second, a tendency towards the fullest freedom of the individual
in the prosecution of all aims, beneficial both for himself and for
society at large. The ideal of the anarchist is thus a mere summing-
up of what he considers to be the next phase of evolution. It is no
longer a matter of faith; it is a matter of scientific discussion . . . '

This doctrine might not seem to differ in any respect from the
aims of laissez-faire liberalism or democratic socialism, but the
anarchist differs profoundly from these political parties in his
conception of means. Any form of government, and particularly
representative government, he sees as a perpetuation of class-rule,
and therefore as conflicting with the necessary evolution of the
individual towards greater potentialities of consciousness and
fullness of life—what Kropotkin called 'the natural growth of
altruistic feelings, which develop as soon as the conditions of life
favour their growth'. That this prospect involved profound problems
of ethics and individual psychology was evident to Kropotkin: his
last work, unfinished, was a treatise on ethics. Its purpose was to
demonstrate that 'the moral sense is a natural faculty in us like the
sense of smell or of touch'. This moral sense arises in the course of
evolution, even within the animal kingdom, and can be expressed
by the one word *solidarity*, that instinct without which, in times of
danger, society would perish.

Kropotkin's insights into the origins of morality have been
powerfully reinforced by the scientific observations of Dr Konrad
Lorenz, 'one of the most distinguished of contemporary ethologists'.
The following passage from his most recent book, *On Aggression**
might have been written by Kropotkin:

'Left to itself, reason is like a computer into which no relevant
information conducive to an important answer has been fed;

* London (Methuen), 1966, pp. 213–14.

logically valid though all its operations may be, it is a wonderful system of wheels within wheels, without a motor to make them go round. The motor power that makes them do so stems from instinctive behaviour mechanisms much older than reason and not directly accessible to rational self-observation. They are the source of love and friendship, of all warmth of feeling, of appreciation of beauty, of the urge to artistic creativeness, of insatiable curiosity striving for scientific enlightenment. These deepest strata of the human personality are, in their dynamics, not essentially different from the instincts of animals, but on their basis human culture has erected all the enormous superstructure of social norms and rites whose function is so closely analogous to that of phylogenetic ritualization.'

The phylogenetically determined principle of mutual aid has been perverted again and again in the course of history, always in the name of some abstract principle—'the abstract trinity of law, religion, and authority'. The anarchist recognizes the danger of all such abstractions: I repeat, he is a pragmatist, or more specifically, a pragmatic realist. He does not believe in any philosophical or political doctrine (not even in anarchism) except in so far as it results in actions that are in accordance with the creative or positive tendencies in human evolution. Ideas and knowledge are instruments in the service of a communal solidarity: aspects of mutual aid. Mutual aid is the only 'phylogenetically adapted mechanism of behaviour' (Lorenz) of a progressive and self-preservative tendency in an evolutionary situation that otherwise is predatory and destructive. It is the predatory tendency, regressive from an evolutionary point of view, that is expressed in the capitalist and *laissez-faire* philosophies of politics.

Anarchism, nevertheless, is highly critical of the scientific attitude as it is usually expressed in politics, which it sees as a threat to liberty. A distinction is made, already by Bakunin, between the exact or natural sciences and 'such sciences as history, philosophy politics, and economic science, which are falsified by being deprived of their true basis, natural science'. With uncanny prescience

Bakunin saw the future development of a State in which the scientist would be enthroned as a despot far more restrictive of the people's liberties than any military despot of the past. 'A scientific body entrusted with the government of society would soon end by devoting itself not to science but to quite another interest. And that, as in the case with all established powers, would consist in its endeavour to perpetuate itself in power and consolidate its position by rendering the society placed in its care even more stupid and consequently even more in need of being governed and directed by such a body.' In this connection Bakunin makes an interesting comparison of science and art:

'Science cannot go outside the realm of abstractions. In this respect it is vastly inferior to art, which, properly speaking, has to do with general types and general situations, but which, by the use of its own peculiar methods, embodies them in forms which, though not living forms in the sense of real life, none the less arouse in our imagination the feeling and recollection of life. In a certain sense it individualizes types and situations which it has conceived; and by means of those individualities without flesh and blood—and consequently permanent and immortal—which it has the power to create, it recalls to our minds living, real individuals who appear and disappear before our eyes. Science, on the contrary, is the perpetual immolation of fugitive and passing, but real life on the altar of eternal abstractions.'*

Much that Bakunin wrote about science seems to anticipate Orwell's *1984*. He accepted science, but he feared scientism, which he saw as almost a branch of Marxism. 'So long as it forms a separate domain, specially represented by a corporation of savants, this ideal world threatens to take the place of the Eucharist in relation to the real world, reserving for its licensed representatives the duties and functions of priests.' This danger could only be avoided 'by

* Bakunin's writings are not easily accessible in English. Unless otherwise stated my quotations come from the excellent anthology compiled and edited by G. P. Maximoff: *The Political Philosophy of Bakunin: Scientific Anarchism*. Glencoe, Illinois (The Free Press) 1953.

means of general education, equally available to all, to dissolve the segregated social organization of science, in order that the masses, ceasing to be a mere herd, led and shorn by privileged shepherds, may take into their own hands their historic destinies'. But writing in 1871 Bakunin did not foresee the immense distance that, nearly a hundred years later, would separate any conceivable form of general education from the specialized arcana of modern science. The sinister combination of scientism and statism can now be broken only by the abolition of the state.

In spite of Bakunin's deep interest in science Kropotkin remains the greatest exponent of a scientific anarchism, but since Kropotkin's time his ideas have been immensely reinforced by the development of individual psychology. To appreciate the relevance of this psychology to anarchism we must return to the philosophical foundations of anarchism and to certain 'stated or assumed premises' of anarchism; they occupy 'a pivotal position' in the Krimerman-Perry anthology, and they are nothing less than the perennial problems of ethical and political philosophy.

These problems—questions of what sort of life men *ought* to live and the sort of society that will permit them to live a life that is both morally imperative and intrinsically desirable, all resolve into the one question of personal freedom (questions of rights and duties, of authority and coercion, are all subordinate to this one concept).

Our anthologists begin by pointing out that Hobbes's definition of liberty as the absence of external impediments would not be acceptable to the anarchist thinkers they present in this section of their book (they include Godwin, Kropotkin, Max Stirner, Nicholas Berdyaev, Adin Ballou and Stephen Pearl Andrews). The anarchist standard of what is ultimately desirable, and of what society should preserve, 'resides in a more constructive ideal which they alternatively designate as "the sovereignty of the individual" (Andrews), "personality" (Berdyaev), "independent judgement" (Godwin), "self-ownership" (Stirner), and so on. Correct or not, this unanimous rejection of the Hobbesian notion of freedom for a more positive chief good provides a unifying theme in anarchist thought.'

My Anarchism

None of the writers quoted in this section of the anthology is specifically a psychologist, unless Stirner's deep and original analysis of the ego is to be called psychological (Freud may have owed something to it). *Der Einzige und sein Eigentum* (*The Ego and his Own**) is a work of considerable power and originality. Marx was so impressed by its threat to his position that he devoted hundreds of pages in *The German Ideology* to its refutation. His attack was so effective that the work has been unjustly neglected ever since, except in Germany (in the margin of Marxist studies) and in France, where in 1904 Victor Basch devoted a comprehensive study to it. More recently Albert Camus paid tribute to it in *L'homme revolté*.† Stirner attacks all ideologies, all concepts and abstractions, all of which without exception demand a surrender of the individual will. The state, of course, above all, for whatever its constitution it is always a despotism, above all when it assumes power in the name of 'the people'. Even freedom is a delusion. 'Who is it that is to become free?', Stirner asks. 'You, I, we. Free from what? From everything that is not you, not I, not we . . . What is left when I have been freed from everything that is not I? Only I; nothing but I. But freedom has nothing to offer to this I himself. Why not proclaim your own identity without further ado? "Freedom" merely awakens your *rage* against everything that is not you; "egoism" calls you to *joy* over yourself, to self-enjoyment. "Freedom" is and remains a *longing*, a romantic plaint, a Christian hope for unearthliness and futurity; "ownness" is a reality, which *of itself* removes just so much unfreedom as by barring your own

* A translation by Steven I. Byington was originally published in 1913. It was reprinted by the Libertarian Press, New York, in 1962.

† Since this essay was written a new work on Stirner has been published in Germany: *Die Ideologie der anonymen Gesellschaft*, by Hans G. Helms (Cologne, Dumont Schauberg Verlag). It runs to more than 600 pages, including a bibliography of 90 pages. Helms sees in Stirner an 'apostle of the middle classes' and a forerunner of fascism, a point of view which can be maintained only by ignoring what is most fundamental in Stirner—his rejection of every kind of ideology. A more balanced view of Stirner's significance may be found in Martin Buber's *Between Man and Man* pp. 40–82. Fontana Library edn., pp. 60–108.

way hinders you. What does not disturb you you will not want to renounce; and, if it begins to disturb you, why, you know that "you must obey yourselves rather than men!" '

Again we see the realism, the anti-idealism that is at base of the anarchist position. Stirner's attack on the State, which is fierce and sustained (and the source of Nietzsche's similar attack), is motivated by this intense feeling that the State establishes and legalizes a mythical entity that deprives the individual of his uniqueness, of his very self. 'What is called a State is a tissue and plexus of dependence and adherence; it is a *belonging together*, a holding together, in which those who are placed together fit themselves to each other; or in short mutually depend on each other; it is the *order* of this *dependence* . . . The State seeks to hinder every free activity by its censorship, its supervision, its police, and holds this hindering to be its duty, because it is in truth a duty of self-preservation. The State wants to make something out of man, therefore there live in it only *made* men; every one who wants to be his own self is its opponent. . .'

What remained in Stirner an affirmation of selfhood and a stubborn opposition to the State in all its collective and repressive aspects has now become a characteristic of the good bourgeois. The modern anarchist tends to ignore the State as an ananchronism which, powerful and intrusive as it is, is destined not so much to wither away, but to become the obvious and indefensible instrument of tyranny, and in this sense it is no longer worth arguing about. The milleniary statists, the scientific 'experts', the professional economists and career politicians, will continue to support it and to extend its powers, but by the people at large the State is now universally hated and from the State's point of view we are all impenitent criminals, tax-evaders and delinquents, or witless citizens waiting to be penned in various social categories or houses of correction—municipal estates, comprehensive schools, hospitals, defence corps, peace corps, collectives of every kind. Against this conception of man has arisen (or rather, has been revived, for in the East it is an ancient doctrine) the conception of man as an individual who becomes whole and even 'godlike' by deliberate dissociation from the collective psyche.

The literature of individual psychology is now immense, and none of it, from Freud and Adler to Jung, Piaget, Rank, Burrow and Fromm can be neglected if we would arrive at an appreciation of its range, its therapeutic pretensions and its effectiveness. It would serve no purpose on the present occasion to discuss the therapeutic aspects of individual psychology; what is relevant is the description of the personal psyche in relation to the collective psyche, and the distinction which Jung in particular makes between the undifferentiated ego instincts and the achieved personality or 'Self'. For the sake of simplicity I shall take Jung's description of the process of 'individuation', which is that part of individual psychology that has most relevance to a philosophy of anarchism.

The individual has, of course, always stood in opposition to the group—to the family group, the environmental group, the tribe and the nation. All psychologists agree that most if not all of the individual's troubles come from mal-adjustment to one or more of these groups, and psycho-therapy has been concerned largely with techniques of reconciliation.

In one direction an extreme mal-adjustment leads to complete alienation and narcissism; in the opposite direction to loss of identity and participation in various forms of mass hysteria. The ideal to be achieved is not so much an uneasy balance between these two tendencies as the achievement of a separate indivisible unity or 'whole', with firm foundations in education and creative activity.

Jung is the best guide to the process because his knowledge is the most eclectic and his exposition the most detailed. An acceptance of the hypothesis of the unconscious (which is the basis of all contemporary psychoanalytic theory and practice) is of course necessary, but the evidence for this is so manifest (in dream activities, for example) and has for so long been the common assumption of all religions and philosophies that we need not pay particular attention to those few mechanists or behaviourists such as H. J. Eysenck who deny its realities—I believe it could be shown that they are merely using a different language to describe identical phenomena.

Jung wrote many (not always consistent) descriptions of the individuation process. The following, long as it is, is the shortest that gives an adequate account of it:

'For the development of personality, then, strict differentiation from the collective psyche is absolutely necessary, since partial or blurred differentiation leads to an immediate melting away of the individual in the collective. There is now a danger that in the analysis of the unconscious the collective and the personal psyche may be fused together, with, as I have intimated, highly unfortunate results. These results are injurious both to the patient's life-feeling and to his fellow men, if he has any influence at all on his environ-ment. Through his identification with the collective psyche he will infallibly try to force the demands of his unconscious upon others, for identity with the collective psyche always brings with it a feeling of universal validity—"godlikeness"—which completely ignores all differences in the personal psyche of his fellows. (The feeling of universal validity comes, of course, from the universality of the collective psyche.) A collective attitude naturally presupposes this same collective psyche in others. But that means a ruthless dis-regard not only of individual differences but also of differences of a more general kind within the collective psyche itself, as for example differences of race. This disregard for individuality obviously means the suffocation of the single individual, as a consequence of which the element of differentiation is obliterated from the community. *The element of differentiation is the individual. All the highest achieve-ments of virtue, as well as the blackest villainies, are individual. The larger a community is, and the more the sum total of collective factors peculiar to every large community rests on conservative prejudices detrimental to individuality, the more will the individual be morally and spiritually crushed, and, as a result, the one source of moral and spiritual progress for society is choked up.* Naturally the only thing that can thrive in such an atmosphere is sociability and whatever is collective in the individual. Everything individual in him goes under, i.e., is doomed to repression. The individual elements lapse into the unconscious, where, by the law of necessity, they are transformed into something essentially baleful, destructive, and anarchical. Socially, this evil principle shows itself in the spectacular crimes—regicide and the like—perpetrated by certain prophetically minded individuals; but in the great mass of the community it remains in the background, and only manifests itself indirectly in the inexorable degeneration of society. *It is a notorious fact that the morality of society as a whole is in inverse ratio to its size; for the greater the aggregation of individuals, the more the individual factors are blotted out, and with them morality, which rests entirely on the moral sense of the individual and the freedom necessary for this.* Hence every man is, in a certain sense, unconsciously a worse man when he is in society than when acting alone; for he is carried by society and to that extent relieved of his individual responsibility. Any large company composed of wholly admirable persons has the morality and intelligence of an unwieldy, stupid and violent animal. The bigger the organization, the more unavoidable is its immorality and blind stupidity (Senatus bestia, senatores boni viri). Society, by automatically stressing all the collective qualities in its individual representatives, puts a premium on mediocrity, on everything that settles down to vegetate in an easy, irresponsible way. Individuality will inevitably be driven to the wall. This process begins in school, continues at the university, and rules all departments in which the State has a hand. In a small social body, the individuality of its members is better safeguarded; and the greater is their relative freedom and the possibility of conscious responsibility. *Without freedom there can be no morality. Our admiration for great organizations dwindles when once we become aware of the other side of the wonder: the tremendous piling up and accentuation of all that is primitive in man, and the unavoidable destruction of his individuality in the interests of the monstrosity that every great organization in fact is.* The man of today, who resembles more or less the collective ideal, has made his heart into a den of murderers, as can easily be proved by the analysis of his unconscious, even though he himself is not in the least disturbed by it. And in so far as he is normally "adapted" to his environment, it is true that the greatest infamy on the part of his group will not disturb him, so long as the majority of his fellows steadfastly believe in the exalted morality of their social organization.'*

I have italicized three passages in this long quotation which seem to have a particular relevance to anarchism—indeed, they might have come from the writings of an anarchist, as might many other passages in Jung's works.† There are just one or two further points that need emphasis if we are to understand the process of individuation.

For example, the emancipated individual cannot wholly escape from the collective psyche, not is it desirable that he should. Jung confesses that he is always astonished to find how much of so-called individual psychology is really collective—'so much, indeed, that the individual traits are completely overshadowed by it. Since, however, individuation is an ineluctable psychological requirement, we can see from the superior force of the collective what very special attention must be paid to this delicate plant "individuality" if it is not to be completely smothered.' But this is just to admit that the process of individuation is a long and severe discipline.

* *Two Essays on Analytical Psychology*, § 240. Trans. by R. F. C. Hull. New York (Bollinger Series), London (Routledge & Kegan Paul), 1953.

† Indeed, Jung sometimes seems to echo Stirner's very words—e.g.: 'Individuation means becoming a single, homogenous being, and, in so far as "individuality" embraces *our innermost, last, and incomparable uniqueness*, it also implies becoming one's own self. We could therefore translate individuation as "coming to selfhood" or "self-realization" '. (*Two Essays*, § 266.) The similarity is, of course, all the more striking in the original German of both writers. It is also interesting to observe that Kropotkin used the word 'individuation' (or 'individualization') long before Jung. Man in an anarchist society, he wrote, 'would be enabled to obtain the full development of all his faculties, intellectual, artistic, and moral, without being hampered by overwork for the monopolists, or by the servility and inertia of mind of the great number. He would thus be able to reach full *individualization* which is not possible either under the present system of *individualism*, or under any system of state-socialism in the so-called *Volkstaat* (popular state)'. (Quoted by Krimerman and Perry, p. 557.)

Secondly, it should be emphasized that individuation does not imply isolation. Jung himself has said: 'Since the individual is not only a single entity, but also, by his very existence, presupposes a collective relationship, the process of individuation does not lead to isolation, but to an intenser and more universal collective solidarity.' This brings us back to Kropotkin and to mutual aid (and to Martin Buber and his concept of 'dialogue'). The ego, we might say, achieves his own in order to offer it, in mutual trust, to 'the other'.

The psychologist (more particularly the psycho-therapist) thinks in terms of a situation that needs correction: his concern is 'the cure of souls'. From a more general sociological point of view the anarchist must think of the process of individuation as an educational one. Krimerman and Perry recognize that anarchism has distinctive and revolutionary implications for education and, indeed, assert that 'no other movement whatever has assigned to educational principles, concepts, experiments, and practices a more significant place in its writings and activities'. Tolstoy is seminal in this respect, but the eleven extracts on education make the most impressive of all the contributions to this anthology, from Godwin to Paul Goodman. Education has been my own particular concern. It is not often realized how deeply anarchist in its orientation a work such as *Education through Art* is and was intended to be. It is of course humiliating to have to confess that its success (and it is by far the most influential book I have written) has been in spite of this fact. I must conclude that I did not make my intention clear enough, but I still hope that the message has been most effective in the degree that it has been most innocently received. My stress in that book was precisely on the individuation of a self—a whole chapter was devoted to 'Unconscious Modes of Integration' and in the first chapter I stated that in my view an answer to the question: *What is the purpose of education?* could only be given within the terms of a libertarian conception of democracy (I should have said 'of socialism', for democracy implies a governmental exercise of power). I then went on to define this purpose as the concurrent development of the 'uniqueness' and the 'social consciousness or reciprocity' of the individual. 'As a result of the infinite permutations of heredity the individual will inevitably be unique, and this uniqueness, because it is something not possessed by anyone else, will be of value to the community.' Uniqueness, I declared, has no *practical* value in isolation. 'One of the most certain lessons of modern psychology, and of recent historical experiences, is that education must be a process, not only of individuation, but also of *integration*, which is the reconciliation of individual uniqueness with social unity.'

I still believe that individuation must proceed *pari passu* with integration, and that an anarchist philosophy must include this concept of reconciliation. Both processes are implicit in Kropotkin's concept of mutual aid, and in Buber's concept of reciprocity (the instinct for communion, *Verbundenheit*). Stirner would have rejected a word like *Verbundenheit*, with its implications of a bond, of a chain on the ego's liberty. But much as anarchism owes to Stirner's realism, and much as we may feel that his philosophical importance has been ignored (Krimerman and Perry point out that it offers 'a possible, and largely ignored, approach to the philosophical problem of free will. If a man does not own the acts he performs, can these be counted as voluntary actions or are they simply responses to factors over which he himself has no control? Can one be held to account for conduct which stems from beliefs and goals, or ideals and interests, of which one is not the owner?') nevertheless we must recognize that the individual is inexorably compelled to find a place in society and undergo some process of integration simple because otherwise he will lapse into schizophrenia. The individual may possess his self, become his 'own', only to find that the result is an intolerable sense of isolation.

All objections to anarchism reduce to the one of impracticality. But none of its critics has considered anarchism as a long-term process of individuation, accomplished by general education and personal discipline—that is to say; from a socio-psychological point of view. I have already noted that Krimerman and Perry come to the conclusion that anarchism must now be regarded as *a consistently individualized pragmatism*, and objections on the score of innate human depravity or selfishness are thus obviated by the anarchist's insistence on reformative education and environmental transformation.

The new interpretation of anarchism now put forward may not seem to differ much from the rational liberalism of Karl Popper, but I think it does so in two ways. In the first place the anarchist cannot abandon the revolutionary myth, much as he may realize with Popper that revolutionary *methods* can only make things worse. Rebellion, as Camus has said, is still today 'at the basis of the struggle. Origin of form, source of real life, it keeps us always erect in the savage formless movement of history.' But rebellion, Camus argued, always demands, defends and recreates moderation. 'Moderation, born of rebellion, can only live by rebellion. It is a perpetual conflict, continually created and mastered by the intelligence.' We cannot do without that tension, that dynamic equilibrium.

In the second place, anarchism differs profoundly from liberalism in its attitude to institutions. The liberal regards institutions as the safeguards of personal liberty. Popper points out, quite truly, that Marxists have been taught to think in terms not of institutions but of classes. 'Classes, however, never rule, any more than nations. The rulers are always certain persons. And, whatever class they may once have belonged to, once they are rulers they belong to the ruling class.' True enough; but what guarantee do we have that the same persons will not exercise a stronger and more tyrannical power under the cover of institutions? Is not that precisely the kind of tyranny we are experiencing now, the tyranny of 'the back-room boys', the faceless 'experts' who control our institutions, our civil service departments, merchant banks, economic councils. Institutions in the modern world are megalomanic, self-perpetuating and viviparous. They do not protect personal liberty: they legalize tyranny and spread its invisible tentacles into every cell of life.

That is why anarchism, however much it may have changed its methods or strategy, remains committed to the non-governmental principle, which implies the breakdown of all centralized institutions —of nations, of federations, of constitutions, of conglomerations of every kind. Not only does the anarchist believe that that government is best that governs least; he does not accept any form of external coercion that prevents the free development of the fully integrated personality. My own belief is that such a development of the personality will never conflict with what Popper calls 'the authority of objective truth'. But finally I must insist with Paul Goodman ('no other contemporary anarchist rivals Paul Goodman in imagination and scholarship') that freedom is not the same thing as *laissez-faire*. Freedom must be understood in a very positive sense: 'it is *the condition of initiating activity* . . . The justification for freedom is that initiation is essential to *any* high-grade human behaviour. Only free action has grace and force'. But free *action*! There is nothing in the anarchist philosophy to justify indifference, complacency, or anything but a pragmatic activity patiently and consistently directed to a revolutionary end.

PART II

VI

T. S. Eliot: A Memoir

In England July 1917 was the deepest and most despairful trough
of the Great World War, but that was the moment chosen to launch
a new illustrated magazine of the arts. An editorial in the first issue
of *Art and Letters* tried to justify this act of defiance. 'Objections
on the score of scarcity of paper and shortage of labour may surely
be overruled when we remember the reams of paper wasted weekly
and the hundreds of compositors daily misemployed on periodicals
which give vulgar and illiterate expression to the most vile and
debasing sentiments.' The self-appointed editor of this periodical,
Frank Rutter, had planned such a venture before the war, when he
was director of the City Art Gallery in Leeds, and it was then and
there, as a student in the University of the same city, that I had met
this now forgotten art critic. He was too old or too unfit to serve in
the army, but when I went to the Front we kept in touch by correspondence and together continued to discuss the project.

A modest paperback volume of poems was published in that same
year 1917 by *The Egoist*, a periodical to which I subscribed. I
immediately acquired *Prufrock and other Observations* and suggested
that its author should be enlisted as a contributor. In the autumn of
that same year I came to London on brief leave from the Front and
during these few days Rutter made contact with the confidential
clerk in Lloyds Bank and we dined together at a restaurant in
Piccadilly Circus called 'The Monico'—it has since disappeared.

The author of *Prufrock* at this time was a very modest young man
of twenty-nine, dressed in a dark city suit. The attitude he adopted

G   97

towards the two people who had been mad enough to launch a new periodical at that particular time was understandably cautious. He himself had recently been appointed literary editor of the other periodical I have mentioned, *The Egoist*, and it had been in its pages, before the publication of *Prufrock*, that I first met his name. But I was devouring every available avant-garde review at that time, so I could have seen it in *The New Age*, to which Ezra Pound had been contributing for some years, or elsewhere.

I still have a distinct image of Eliot as he sat between us, his back to the wall. The restaurant had a faded pseudo-rococo elegance, but what war-time fare we were offered I cannot remember. I was excited and indifferent to food. I had been that very day to Buckingham Palace to receive a medal (the justification of my leave from the Front) and I was exhilarated, not so much by that honour, which I affected to despise, as by the feeling of escape from the horrors of the trenches, by the unaccustomed warmth and luxury, by the sudden plunge into an atmosphere of art and letters. Eliot was no doubt a little abashed by the apparition of a young hero

> aus dem zerstampften gefild
> Heil aus dem prasselnden guss

and was anxious to make excuses for his own civilian status—he had, he explained, made an application for a commission in the Naval Reserve, but had waited in vain for his call-up. I was merely amused by his scruples—I was already a pacifist in spirit and my only wish was to see the end of the war and the beginning of a new life devoted to literature.

A promise of collaboration was given, with perhaps a slight reserve that might have been critical of enthusiasm of any kind or, as my subsequent knowledge of his personality would rather indicate, some cautious strategy. In the years to come, when we had become close friends, he would often recommend caution—caution in showing one's hand too soon, caution in speech and correspondence, caution in the small exchanges of literary life. 'Always', he would say, 'acknowledge the gift of a book before there has been time to read it: if you wait you have to commit yourself to an opinion.' One of his rules was never to contribute to the first number of a new periodical—wait to see what company you are going to keep.

There was no contribution, therefore, in the first two or three issues of *Art and Letters*. The war dragged on and publication became more difficult. It was not until the Spring issue of 1919 that his first contribution, an essay on Marivaux, appeared. In the next number (Summer 1919) "Burbank with a Baedeker" and "Sweeney Erect" were printed, and this number includes an essay by Ezra Pound on De Bosschère. To the Autumn issue of that same year Eliot contributed "Notes on the Blank Verse of Christopher Marlowe"; to the next number "The Duchess of Malfi and Poetic Drama" and finally, to the Spring number of 1920, "Euripides and Gilbert Murray".

Art and Letters did not survive beyond the year 1920. In its later stages it was edited by Osbert Sitwell—still in association with Frank Rutter. After the war I had taken up a post in the Treasury, which was not compatible with journalistic activities, so I kept in the background. The magazine had been a brave effort—it published articles, stories and poems by all the Sitwells, by Richard Aldington, Wyndham Lewis, Ford Madox Hueffer, Aldous Huxley, Ronald Firbank, Katherine Mansfield and Wilfred Owen. It reproduced drawings and paintings by Picasso, Matisse, Modigliani, Gaudier Brzeska and Wyndham Lewis. But it lost money and went the way of all such brave efforts in a philistine world. Its significance is that it was in some sense a forerunner of *The Criterion*. My acquaintance with Eliot, in the years immediately after the war ripened to friendship slowly but surely. Eliot married and brought his pretty vivacious wife to the Saturday afternoon tea-parties given by Helen Rootham and Edith Sitwell in their Bayswater apartment. The euphoria of our first meeting had faded: the soldier had become a civil servant, but one who was still busy with literary projects. It was Osbert Sitwell, who was free and comparatively wealthy, who assumed the leadership, and it was the Sitwells, as a trio, who made the pace for us all. Pound disappeared towards the end of 1920, ostensibly disgusted with British philistinism but really because he found no place in post-war England. It may be doubted if he ever understood the English—certainly not typical eccentrics like the Sitwells. But the Sitwells were genuinely English; their rejection of British philistinism was as absolute as Ezra's, but they wished to concentrate their forces on the home front—they were indifferent to Ezra's troubadours and symbolists. And Ezra was in the first place committed to Harriet Monroe and later to Margaret Anderson. He was exporting what little talent he could find to America, and that helped no one in England. If he had any local allegiance it was to that oddity *The Egoist*, and it was he who in 1917 had persuaded its owners, Harriet Weaver and Dora Marsden, to appoint Eliot as literary editor. Not that the post gave him much scope, for its primary object was to publish Dora Marsden's esoteric philosophy, and though eventually space was found for the serial publication of Joyce's *Ulysses*, the literary contents were usually limited to a short poem or two, an article on music, and two or three reviews of books.

The Sitwells were apt to make fun of Ezra—indeed, it was very difficult for anyone to take him seriously in person (that is to say, the *persona* he used to project). Apart from his exotic appearance, he rattled off his elliptic sentences with a harsh nasal twang, twitched incessantly and prowled round the room like an insulted panther. He was not made for compromise or cooperation, two qualities essential for any literary or artistic 'movement'. He disappeared, first to Paris and then to Rapallo, and the place he might have occupied in the post-war literary scene in London was quietly assumed by Eliot.

It was quietly assumed by a man who had lost all superficial trace of his American origin and who had already decided that his spiritual home was in England. The complexities involved in this decision were not to be appreciated by a true-born Englishman, but I was aware of the struggle that was going on in Eliot's mind. 'Some day', he wrote to me on St George's Day, 1928 (his own inscription),

T. S. Eliot: A Memoir

'I want to write an essay about the point of view of an American who wasn't an American, because he was born in the South and went to school in New England as a small boy with a nigger drawl, but who wasn't a southerner in the South because his people were northerners in a border state and looked down on all southerners and Virginians, and who so was never anything anywhere and who therefore felt himself to be more a Frenchman than an American and more an Englishman than a Frenchman and yet felt that the U.S.A. up to a hundred years ago was a family extension. It is almost too difficult even for H.J. who for that matter, wasn't an American at all, in that sense.'

By this time Eliot had become an Englishman in legal fact, and apart from the occasion of our first meeting in 1917, when the war situation was compelling him to acknowledge his Americanness, or on one or two later occasions when in a mood of solemn gaiety he would sing a ballad like "The Reconstructed Rebel", I was never conscious that he was in any way less English than myself. From the first he fitted naturally into English clothes and English clubs, into English habits generally. In fact, if anything gave him away it was an Englishness that was a shade too correct to be natural.

It is difficult, especially for someone not blessed with a good memory, to reconstruct the events between the end of the war and the foundation, in 1923, of *The Criterion*. From that year Eliot was our undisputed leader. I imply the formation of a party, of a 'new front', and that was indeed the intention, as the 'commentaries' in *The Criterion* soon made clear. *Art and Letters* had come to an end mainly for financial reasons, and from that moment (the summer of 1920) the foundation of a new and better magazine was constantly discussed whenever we foregathered. There were by then three centres of intellectual ferment: the so-called Bloomsbury Group; the poets associated with Harold Monro and his review *Poetry and Drama*; and the Sitwells, who still carried on a campaign against the literary establishment (the Squirearchy as it was sometimes called, for its most prominent member was J. C. Squire). Middleton

Murry should perhaps be mentioned, but though he was latter to found *The Adelphi* and gather round him the disciples of D. H. Lawrence, he never came to terms with Eliot (though he enormously respected him as a critic) nor with modern poetry (his own poetry is the best evidence of that). He was also of an older generation and he never seemed to understand the poetic revolution that began with *Prufrock*.

Nor did Harold Monro, for all his eager devotion to poetry as a cause and to Eliot as a friend. It is a melancholy fact that he had rejected *Prufrock* when it was offered to him for publication by the Poetry Bookshop. As the years passed and Eliot's prestige grew he became somewhat embittered, and though we all attended the parties he gave at the Bookshop, we knew that in some sense he was not with us.

Nor, of course, was the Bloomsbury Group. Leonard and Virginia Woolf, who were the real heart of that group, were very devoted to Eliot, and it was they who, as the Hogarth Press, published not only the *Poems* of 1920, but the first edition of *The Waste Land* in 1922. But the publications of the Hogarth Press, which were actually composed and printed in the cellar of Woolf's house in Richmond, were in no sense representative of the Bloomsbury Group, and whatever the possessive attitude of Bloomsbury-ites such as Clive Bell may have been, the truth is that Eliot carefully kept his distance. The obituary of Virginia which he wrote for *Horizon* shocked us all by its chilly detachment.

There was no other group that mattered. There was Orage, in some respect the most effective catalyst of the period, but the *New Age*, which for several years provided Pound with an outlet, was now given over to Social Credit (with Pound as a convert) and to the doctrines of Gurdjieff (which were too esoteric even for Pound). There were anonymous institutions like *The Times Literary Supplement*, and its editor, Bruce Richmond, deserves to be remembered as one who quickly appreciated the new talents that were forming round Eliot and gave them substantial encouragement in his columns (the early reviews of *Prufrock* and *Poems 1920* should not be remembered against him; no one, in the years to come, regretted them more).

Such was the literary situation in 1923 when Eliot, aided by a subsidy from Lady Rothermere, decided that the time was ripe to launch a review. He took his time and chose his team with great deliberation. The group that rallied round him was unique in that it never questioned his leadership—but there were two that held back: Richard Aldington, who had developed an intense jealousy of Eliot, and Wyndam Lewis, who though pressed by Eliot to collaborate, preferred to cut his own aggressive swathe. For myself it soon became a question of deep personal devotion, and Eliot responded with a confidence which I have valued more than anything else in my life.

I will now try to describe the personal relationship that developed between Eliot and myself over a period of nearly fifty years. It will not be easy and it will involve some confessions that are not altogether creditable to myself.

When I first met Eliot I was, from an intellectual point of view, both ignorant and *naïf*. I had not had the advantage of his orderly education and philosophical training. The only credit I might claim was the experience of war, and though he respected this, I was in the process of disowning it. The pacifism that had become a deep conviction for me was to be one of the few areas of mutual misunderstanding. The reasons which led Eliot to reject pacifism were perfectly logical, whereas it was war itself that had given me the right to be illogical and angry. But neither this issue, nor the many issues bound up with it (the whole complex of humanism and romanticism) ever threatened our devotion to each other. I do not know what he found to like or respect in someone so fundamentally different in background and temperament, but first my Englishness, I suppose. My naïvety, even after the experience of war, was that of a country boy, uncorrupted by society or learned sophistication. The enthusiasm that had survived a war was but another aspect of this same naïvety, and Eliot must have been aware that it embraced him with an intuitive sympathy and understanding. This poet, in spite of his reserve, was not indifferent to devotion, and he felt the need for one or two disciples.

The illusion that I might become one was fostered for a time by my editing of the posthumous papers of T. E. Hulme. I do not think that Hulme's *Speculations*, when they were published in 1924, made any difference to Eliot's political idealism or philosophical faith, but his convictions were immensely strengthened. As the man who had rescued Hulme from a probable oblivion I had earned Eliot's deep gratitude. At first he must have assumed that I could only have undertaken such an unremunerative task from some sense of intellectual affinity, whereas in fact I had done the work to oblige Orage, who had been entrusted with the task by Hulme's executors. Orage had been very kind to me as a young aspiring writer, and when he suggested (perhaps a little disingenuously) that the editing of Hulme's papers would be an educative experience for me, I agreed, not realizing (though I had often read Hulme's contributions to *The New Age*) what a bombshell I was innocently manufacturing.

From 1919 to 1922 I was an Assistant Principal in the Treasury, a position that meant I could not publicly take part in activities such as journalism that might be held to compromise my official duties. For this reason, though I was in effect an editor of *Art and Letters*, my name never appeared on the title-page. But in 1922 I left the Treasury for a more congenial post in the Victoria and Albert Museum. I was still a civil servant, but provided I was discreet no one would object to my literary activities. The transfer coincided more or less with the foundation of *The Criterion* and with Eliot's resignation from the city bank. Since Eliot's time was now more elastic than mine, and in order to preserve a regular contact, it was agreed that we should meet for lunch one day every week in South Kensington and for the next seven years we foregathered at a pub called 'The Grove' in Beauchamp Place. 'The Grove' became a Mermaid Tavern to which, week by week (I think it was every Thursday) came not only some of the regular contributors to *The Criterion*, but also any sympathising critics or poets from abroad who might be visiting London. The 'regulars', apart from Eliot and myself, were F. S. Flint, Frank Morley, Bonamy Dobrée (absent in Egypt part of the time), and one or more of my museum colleagues.

But these lunches were not *The Criterion* meetings. These took place in the evening, about once a month, and usually in a small private room at the Ristorante Commercio in Soho. Their purpose was not so much to discuss business as to introduce contributors to one another, to exchange ideas and to build up some kind of 'phalanx' whose unity would be reflected in the pages of the magazine. I doubt if they achieved this purpose, but they were enjoyable and intellectually stimulating. They were in no way dominated by the editor; they were not very serious. On such occasions Eliot often revealed a gay and even hilarious spirit far different from his normal demeanour.

'My conception of leader or "organizer" (he wrote to me in a letter which is undated but apparently of October, 1924) is simply of a necessary organ in a body, which has no superiority at all, but exercises a particular function, and makes it possible for others to do their best work.' This is the 'conception' he maintained during all the years of his editorship of *The Criterion*. The letter is a long one, and includes an 'apologia' which perhaps I should quote because it shows how early Eliot had formulated certain principles of personal conduct which he was to maintain for the next forty years:

The ideal which you propose in your letter is very near to that which I proposed to myself when I undertook the review, and which I have kept in mind ever since. The ideal which was present to the mind of Lady Rothermere at the beginning was that of a more chic and brilliant Art and Letters, which might have a fashionable vogue among a wealthy few. I had and have no resentment against her for this, as I have no criticism to make of her conduct throughout: she has given me a pretty free hand, has been quite as appreciative as one could expect a person of her antecedents and connexions to be, and the game between us has been a fair one. I have I think given her as much as possible of what she wants, and she has given me the possibility of an organ. It is true that I have laid myself open to the censure both of persons who assumed that I was making money out of the work, and of those who knew that I was taking nothing for it—and who consequently believe that I am running the paper for other discreditable reasons—which latter group of persons, by the way, includes my relatives in America. One does not like to explain oneself only to arouse the accusation of hypocrisy, to be associated with the other causes of impeachment, and one learns to keep silence. I have another reason for keeping silence, and that is that I find that I sometimes give people an impression of arrogance and intolerant self-conceit. If I say generally that I wish to form a 'phalanx', a hundred voices will forthwith declare that I wish to be a leader, and that my vanity will not allow me to serve, or exist on terms of equality with others. If one maintains a cause, one is either a fanatic or a hypocrite: and if one has any definite dogmas, then one is imposing those dogmas upon those who cooperate with one.

I wish, certainly, to get as homogeneous a group as possible: but I find that homogeneity is in the end indefinable: for the purposes of the Criterion, it cannot be reduced to a creed of numbered capitals. I do *not* expect everyone to subscribe to all the articles of my own faith, or to read Arnold, Newman, Bradley, or Maurras with my eyes. It seems to me that at the present time we need more dogma, and that one ought to have as precise and clear a creed as possible, when one thinks at all: but a creed is always in one sense smaller than the man, and in another sense larger; one's formulations never fully explain one, although it is necessary to formulate: I do not, for myself, bother about the apparent inconsistency—which has been made the most of—between my prose and my verse. Why then should I bother about particular differences of formulation between myself and those whom I should like to find working with me?

This is to make a little clearer my notion of a phalanx. When I *write*, I must write to the limit of my own convictions and aspirations: but I don't want to impose these on others, any more than I should be willing to reduce myself to the common denominator of my colleagues. What is essential is to find those persons who have an impersonal loyalty to some faith not antagonistic to my own.

Here we have the demand for 'an impersonal loyalty'—loyalty not to an individual, not even to a political or critical programme, but to 'some faith not antagonistic to my own'. Eliot in this letter went on to discuss persons, possible contributors, and they range from conservatives such as Charles Whibley to modernists such as Edwin Muir. Always there is the assumption that I am by his side, an aide-de-camp in 'what might easily become a heart-breaking struggle'. My own faith was judged as certainly not antagonistic to his own. But what was my own faith?

It was to be defined, tentatively, in the volume of essays which Eliot asked me to prepare for the first list of the reorganized firm of Faber & Gwyer (later Faber & Faber) which he had joined as an editorial director. This book, *Reason and Romanticism*, was published in 1926, and though the Reason of it owes something to Hulme and even more to Eliot, the Romanticism was my own. It was already my declared purpose to seek some reconciliation or 'synthesis' of these opposed faiths. If Eliot had any desire to check me at that time, it was all done with a very gentle rein, and our intimacy became closer week by week. At this period, 1926–31, we were seeing each other so frequently that the correspondence is sparse, and I am thrown back on my imperfect memory to recover the immediacy of the events. All those years I commuted to a suburb of London and in 1926 built myself a house near Beaconsfield, about twenty-five miles to the west of London. The station for Beaconsfield is Marylebone, and Clarence Gate Gardens, the block of flats to which Eliot returned about 1927 or 1928, was a few hundred yards from this terminus. It became convenient to dine with the Eliots occasionally before catching a train to the country.

Before this, however, Eliot and Vivienne had lived for a number of years in a small house at 57 Chester Terrace, in that part of London that hesitates between Belgravia and Chelsea. After the Criterion dinners, which generally lasted too long for me to catch my last train home, I would sometimes spend the night at Chester

Terrace. I remember how on one such occasion I woke early and presently became conscious that the door of my room, which was on the ground floor, was slowly and silently being opened. I lay still and saw first a hand and then an arm reach round the door and lift from a hook the bowler hat that was hanging there. It was a little before seven o'clock and Mr Eliot was on his way to an early communion service. It was the first intimation I had had of his conversion to the Christian faith.

This reticence was maintained in all his private affairs. I was a close witness of the tragic progress of his first marriage. Vivienne was a frail creature and had not been married long before she began to suffer from serious internal ailments. These exasperated an already nervous temperament and she slowly but surely developed the hysterical psychosis to which she finally succumbed. Eliot's sufferings in these years were acute, but only once did he unburden himself to me. This was in a letter which I received while I was on a short holiday in Sussex, but this particular letter has disappeared— it is possible that I was asked to destroy it. Posterity will probably judge Vivienne harshly, but I remember her in moments when she was sweet and vivacious; later her hysteria became embarrassing. My own first marriage was to break up under very similar circumstances and that too, as time passed, increased our mutual sympathy. Eliot, however, could not accept my drastic solution of the problem, which was the dissolution of the marriage. Though eventually legally separated, he remained single so long as his first wife was alive.

His moral rectitude, though explicit, was never unctuous. In conversation he would freely express his disapproval of the conduct of his friends, but I do not remember that he ever brought a friendship to an end on such grounds. He would often 'demur' to some line of action (a letter to the press, for example, on some political issue) but I was only reproved once with something like sternness. This was ten years ago. Wyndham Lewis had published a pamphlet called *The Demon of Progress in the Arts* which contained a malicious and I thought at the time a treacherous attack on me. It came as a surprise because I had known Lewis since 1917, and though I had never felt quite at ease with him (who ever did?) I admired him both as a painter and as a writer. In the year in question, 1949, the Institute of Contemporary Arts, of which I was President, had organized an exhibition called "Forty Thousand Years of Modern Art", and the selection committee, of which I was not a member, had chosen two early abstract paintings by Lewis, belonging to a private collector. Lewis heard of this and I immediately received from him telegrams and registered letters protesting against what he considered a deliberate misrepresentation of his status as an artist. Very reluctantly, on my request, the committee agreed to withdraw the pictures, but the incident continued to rankle in Lewis's schizophrenic mind (I use a clinical expression, but it had for long been obvious that Lewis suffered from what, in less clinical language, we call a persecution complex).

My answer to this attack was a lecture delivered at the Institute of Contemporary Arts which I called "The Psychopathology of Reaction in the Arts". I did not wish to indulge in personal polemics so I carefully avoided any mention of Lewis's name, discussing in general terms the 'case' of the artist who renounces his early revolutionary fervour to become a reactionary in later life—I gave Wordsworth as a typical example.

My subtlety misfired—practically nobody identified my remarks with Lewis, so when the *Sewanee Review* published the lecture in the Fall of 1955 I added a footnote which was meant to be ironical but would reveal my target to anyone who had read Lewis's pamphlet. I should add that before this, on the basis of the script of my lecture, Eliot had made some objections which were fair enough and meant to safeguard his own position. In a letter of 16 September 1955 he had written:

'I still do not think, however, that you have made clear enough the distinction between your *general* use of "reactionary" in contrast to "conservative" (a distinction which has only to be drawn to be accepted). In the former sense, the term applies to Charles Maurras, for example. In the latter sense it is either your own invention, or is perhaps borrowed from psychologists: in either case, it seems to me to need more explicit definition for the general reader. And of course I am still very doubtful about the propriety of the psychological approach in such a controversy. ****** ******, of course, is in his own way as much a "case" as Lewis; but wouldn't it be better to ignore what they say than to rebut them on that ground? A man's mental kinks may very well account for his being wrong; but should not one first meet him on his own ground and prove that he is wrong, before explaining how he came to be wrong?'

I thought that that was exactly what I had done. In any case, it was too late to withdraw (my lecture had meanwhile been issued as a pamphlet by the I.C.A.). But this first rebuke was mild compared with the sternness that followed the publication of the lecture in the *Sewanee Review*. The ironical footnote caused Eliot 'a fresh shock', as he says in a letter of 14 November, and 'I shall have to take a little time to perpend and decide what, if anything, I have to say further'. I waited like a condemned criminal for my sentence and it came five days later in the following letter:

19 November 1955.

Dear Herbert,

I have no desire to prolong our recent correspondence, and I should like to be able, after writing this letter, to close the subject altogether. But your letter of the 12th made me realize that I could not have made my position clear, and I want to do so, defining the issue with which I have been concerned.

My interest in this discussion has not been in Wyndham Lewis personally, or in his personal disagreement with you, or in opposed views of modern art. In such matters, I should certainly not intervene: I would not enter the lists with artists and art critics. What first interested me was a question arising out of Wyndham Lewis's book and your pamphlet: the question of the legitimacy and the question of the wisdom (two distinct but related questions) of the use of psychological artillery in a battle of this kind. This is a fascinating question, which I should like to take up some day, in a cooler atmosphere; but it is not germane to my recent perplexity. This arose solely from the fact that our conversation on the subject, and the content of your letter of the 18th September, gave me reason to suppose that the origin of your pamphlet was the need which you felt to reply to Lewis, that a direct rebuttal would be futile, and that the form of reply you had adopted was an analysis of a psychological type, as instances of which you told me you had Lewis and Chirico in mind. You will therefore judge of my surprise on reading, in the Sewanee Review, the explicit statement that your article—to which you had given the new title of "The Lost Leader" —had no application to Lewis. And your letter of November 12 didn't succeed in clearing away my bewilderment.

That's all there is to it. And I hope, after so many years' friendship, that you will always be equally frank with me when you find my published words unsatisfying.

Yours ever
Tom

I defended myself to the best of my ability and ten years later I still think that the best answer to a malicious attack is a cool analysis of the state of mind that occasions it. But the footnote was a mistake: if I had wanted to implicate Lewis in my argument I should have done so openly. It was naïve to imagine that the public would join in a game of blind man's buff.

Eliot was to add his own ironic footnote. On one of the last occasions that I lunched with him alone at the Garrick Club, he confessed that in his life there had been few people whom he had found it impossible to like, but that Lewis was one of them. What should be realized, by anyone who wishes to understand the complexity of Eliot's moral conscience, is that he could be fiercely loyal to people whose 'faith' he respected but whom he could not love.

Perhaps he could be equally loyal to people he loved but did not respect, and I may have come into this category as time passed and our opinions continued to diverge. When he announced in the preface to *For Lancelot Andrews* (1928) that he was a classicist in literature, a royalist in politics and an anglo-catholic in religion, I could only retort that I was a romanticist in literature, an anarchist in politics and an agnostic in religion. But such a statement of differences he could respect; what he could not tolerate was any false interpretation of the position he himself held. I remember one occasion of this kind. In the first edition of my autobiography, *Annals of Innocence and Experience* (1940) there was a sentence, or part of one, to which he took strong exception: '. . . it is a genuine puzzle to me how anyone with a knowledge of the comparative history of religions can retain an exclusive belief in the tenets of his particular sect'. This led to some earnest discussion, but I see that the only correction I made in subsequent editions was to italicize the word 'exclusive', with an intention that now escapes me. It may be, however, that the original objection was to the sentence as it appeared in the typescript or proofs of the book, which Eliot would have seen as a director of Faber & Faber.

I now want to get a little closer to the nature of this poet I knew so well for so many years, but I begin with an overwhelming sense of the complexity of the subject, and of my inadequacy to deal with it perceptively. One's first fear is that one may be reading an intellectual refinement, a subtlety of mind and thought, into the personality of a man who was fundamentally simple. There is no necessary correspondence between thought and personality: a man of very simple habits, such as Kant, can be master of a very complex philosophy. But Eliot was certainly not a Kant. It is true that he led a comparatively sedate life: he too was regular in his habits and punctilious in his manners—he even held that regular habits were conducive to poetic creation, in this, as in so much else, agreeing with Coleridge, 'the sad ghost' that beckoned him from the shades. He loved his office work at Faber's, and kept up his duties there long after there was any need to do so—though by nature he was apt to be cautious in financial matters. He was never mean, but he was not extravagant—he would take a bus or a tube in preference to a taxi if the cheaper service were easily available. He lived comfortably in town apartments and would never have indulged in that last infirmity of a romantic temperament, a country house. He was, in fact, a townsman by preference and never at ease in the country. He might enjoy a holiday in the south of France or, in his later years, in the West Indies, but he was not a traveller by choice and often reproved me for my cultural peregrinations (he thought that activities like lecturing and reviewing should be kept within strict bounds. A poet, he said, should not write reviews after the age of thirty-five—indeed, he did not approve of reviewing at any time as distinct from the writing of critical essays). He had a positive distaste for the weekly critical journals and boasted that he had never contributed to *The New Statesman*.

He had, as is well known, a thorough education in philosophy, but he did not parade his knowledge of the subject. He would occasionally refer to Bradley, and more often, in an anecdotic fashion, to his Oxford tutor in philosophy, Harold Joachim. But mainly, if we were in a literary mood, our talk would be quite general, concerned with our work, our friends, and the gossip of the day. As the years passed he became just a little pontifical, and would refer to his own writings in a tone of voice that was a shade too solemn. He would use expressions like 'Valéry, Yeats and I'—with perfect justice, but one was rather checked by the calm acceptance of a status that one felt should be left to others to confer.

Of classical authors he undoubtedly felt most affinity for Dante; his appreciation of Shakespeare and all the Romantic poets was subject to his moral or religious scruples. He knew perfectly well that a good poet is not necessarily a good Christian; nevertheless, he maintained that the poet, as a member of a Christian community, must be judged by the moral standards of that community. This brought him nearer to a man whom I believe he honoured above all other English writers—Samuel Johnson, with whom he shared a faith in God and the fear of death. Johnson, both as a poet and as a critic, was constantly in his mind, and he had a factual knowledge of Boswell's *Life* that enabled him to play a game of quiz with fellow

Johnsonians like Frank Morley—a game that could become rather tedious to the uninitiated. The same game, on a somewhat more frivolous level, was played with the complete works of Conan Doyle, and (more arcanely) with the complete works of Wilkie Collins. I once earned his surprised admiration by answering some ploy of this kind with a quotation from *Poor Miss Finch*, a novel by Collins which my wife had picked up at a country auction. I had opened it idly and read with amusement that the heroine's father, a politician from South America, had 'succumbed to his seventeenth revolution', a beautiful phrase that had stuck in my mind.

His admiration for his contemporaries was limited and uncertain. I have mentioned his loyalty to Lewis. Eliot once publicly committed himself to the opinion that Lewis wrote the best prose style of our time, the truth being that there was nothing to recommend it except its occasional vivid brutality. To James Joyce he was completely devoted, both to the writer and to the man. He helped him in many practical ways, and even remitted in his case his moral sanctions. His relations with Pound are clear from the published correspondence. Again, Eliot was always solicitous for the personal welfare of a friend to whom he felt he owed a great debt. But if the reader would like to appreciate how clinically cool Eliot could be even to the best of his friends, one he had called 'probably the most important living poet in our language', he should read the two pages devoted to Pound in *After Strange Gods*. If Shakespeare and Shelley are not to be spared the moral criterion, there was no reason to spare 'poor Ezra'.

This firm assertion of a moral criterion (the criterion of *The Criterion*) has to be accepted as the key to Eliot's character (his *character* and not his personality, but that distinction of mine was precisely the one he could not accept). Once the finality of that criterion was accepted it could be ignored—it never stood in the way of the most affectionate relationships with heretics or pagans like Pound and myself. And yet one always had a slight uneasiness in his presence, fearing that he might at any moment assume the judicial robes. If Shelley's ideas could be dismissed as 'shabby' and most of his verse as 'bad jingling', where, in Mr Eliot's final judgement, did we stand?

It has been said that this moralistic attitude, which was extended to all forms of liberalism, must necessarily have put Eliot on the side of autocracy and, not to evade the word that has been used, fascism. This is not true. In all the years I knew him I never heard him express any sympathy for either Mussolini or Hitler—from his point of view they were godless men. 'The fundamental objection to fascist doctrine', he once wrote, 'the one that we conceal from our-selves because it might condemn ourselves, is that it is pagan.' He did not believe in democracy, and who can blame him? He believed in 'a community of Christians', and when it came to a close dis-cussion of what he meant by this ideal, it seemed to have more in common with my anarchism than with any form of autocracy. He believed in a hierarchy, but he also believed in 'roots' (see his Introduction to Simone Weil's *The Need for Roots* which he wrote at my suggestion), and above all he believed in tradition. He knew that the values he cherished could not exist in the modern state, democratic or totalitarian.

He has been accused of anti-semitism, but again I never heard such sentiments from his own lips. I know that there are one or two phrases in his writings that lend some substance to this accusation, but all of us, if we are honest with ourselves, must confess to a certain spontaneous xenophobia. It is an instinct that the educated man controls or eradicates, and in this respect Eliot was as controlled as the best of us.

Perhaps too controlled for general converse. From the beginning there was a withholding of emotion, a refusal to reveal the inner man. I always felt myself in the presence of a remorseful man, of one who had some secret sorrow or guilt. What I took for remorse may not have had its origins in personal experience; a feeling of guilt may be caused by a realization of 'the all-consuming power of original sin'. This Eliot, like Kierkegaard, certainly possessed.

His emotional reserve may have had a remoter cause—after all, he had had a puritannical background in his childhood. I know that

my own reserved nature, which I inherit from my Yorkshire
ancestry, is often mistaken for an absence of feeling or sympathy;
whereas, to paraphrase one of Eliot's own well-known aphorisms,
only the man who feels deeply experiences the need to hide his
feelings. So long as she was alive Eliot must have felt very close to
his mother, but he never talked about her, and when he published
her 'dramatic poem' *Savonarola* (the volume is not dated, but I
think it was about 1925-6), he handed a copy to me with a depre-
catory gesture. The Introduction he wrote for this volume is again
an impersonal document, devoted to 'History and Truth' and 'Of
Dramatic Form' and telling us nothing directly about the authoress.
Indirectly we may gather that she was a disciple of Schleiermacher,
Emerson, Channing and Herbert Spencer; that she was (or might
have been) a contributor to the *Hibbert Journal*; and that she was
opposed to ecclesiasticism. All this, we are told, can be deduced
from the text of the play, which renders 'a state of mind contemporary with the author'. The condemned Savonarola in his cell
utters these words:

> This is the Hall that grew with my desire
> And quick-winged words that flew like shafts of fire

Change 'Hall' (the Hall of the Grand Council) to 'Hell' and we have
words that strangely anticipate the 'flame of incandescent terror' in
'Little Gidding';

> We only live, only suspire
> Consumed by either fire or fire.

I must now draw this brief memoir to an end, with the realization
that I have completely failed to convey the nature and the presence
of this great man. I have said that he was inaccessible, but perhaps
some other friends were luckier than I and found intimacy as well as
loyalty and affection. I shall probably wait in vain for such revela-
tions, and, to tell the truth, they would not make any difference to
my knowledge of the man. The man I knew, in all his reserve, was
the man he wished to be: a serious but not necessarily a solemn man,

a severe man never lacking in kindness and sympathy, a *profound* man (profoundly learned, profoundly poetic, profoundly spiritual). And yet to outward appearance a correct man, a conventional man, an infinitely polite man—in brief, a gentleman. He not only was not capable of a mean deed; I would also say that he never had a mean thought. He could mock folly and be severe with sin, and there were people he simply did not wish to know. But his circle of friends, though never very large, was very diverse, and he could relax with great charm in the presence of women. He had moods of gaiety and moods of great depression—I have known occasions when I left him feeling that my spirit had been utterly depleted. Often he was witty (in a somewhat solemn voice); his anecdotes were related with great deliberation. He did not hesitate to discuss policies or person-alities, but he condemned idle gossip (of the kind typical of the Bloomsbury set). In personal habits he was scrupulously correct and clean, never a Bohemian in thought or appearance; but he had a streak of hypochondria, and was addicted to pills and potions. He had good reason for taking care of himself, for he easily took a chill and often suffered from a distressing cough. I never saw him indulge in any sport. One weekend he spent with me early in our friendship (it was 1927 or 1928) he came clad in a most curious pair of checkered breeches, neither riding-breeches nor 'plus-fours', but some hybrid which was certainly not from Saville Row. He made a fetish of umbrellas, as is perhaps well-known. He had them specially made with enormous handles, with the excuse that no one would take such an umbrella from a cloakroom by mistake. He relished good food and beer and wine, but his speciality was cheese, of which he had tasted a great many varieties. I think I gained a point in his esteem because I came from a region responsible for Wensleydale, 'the Mozart of cheeses'. At his club the cheeseboard would be pro-duced with great solemnity and the quality or maturity of the cheeses tested before being offered to his guests.

In all affairs he was a man of taste, but taste, like tradition, is acquired. I do not think he had any direct sensuous appreciation of the visual arts. After our lunch at 'The Grove' he would sometimes return to the Museum with me to see some particular treasure I had mentioned, but he did not respond to such things with more than a respectful curiosity. I rarely discussed contemporary art with him, and though I once or twice tried to establish some personal contact between him and artists like Henry Moore and Ben Nicholson, my efforts came to little or nothing. If pressed he would no doubt have admitted that the tradition that led from Poe and Baudelaire to Laforgue and Rimbaud and his own poetry could not be entirely divorced from the tradition that led from Delacroix and Cézanne to Matisse and Picasso, but he would not himself have made much of the comparison.

It might be asked finally whether such a great poet ever discussed poetry, and the answer is No if we mean poetry in general (that he reserved for his books). He would often consult me about particular poets who wished to be published by Fabers, and we freely discussed the relative merits of our contemporaries, English and American. In the early years he would sometimes show me the draft or proofs of one of his own poems and invite my criticism, but this less and less as the years went by. He sometimes commented on poems I had written and his criticism was always practical and acute, concerned with the meaning of words or some infelicity of phrase. He never expressed any general opinion about my poetry, though he often blamed me for neglecting poetry for art criticism and other non-poetic activities. I knew, however, that I had some measure of his esteem—after all, he sponsored the publication of my poems with Fabers. I have mentioned his self-esteem, without questioning his perfect right to it; but this was an attitude to which, as a poet, I could only oppose a self-effacing modesty. I once wrote a poem which, after I had written it, I realized had perfectly described our relationship as poets—a poem in the Chinese manner called "Lu Yun's Lament", but neither Eliot nor, as far as I know, anyone else ever saw its application. Like my footnote on Wyndham Lewis, it was ironic to the point of irrelevance.

The most significant of all Eliot's poems, from a confessional point of view, is "The Hollow Men". It was written in 1925, the year of religious crisis, and apart from some minor poems, it is the last example of what I would call his *pure* poetry. "Ash Wednesday" which followed in 1930, is already a moralistic poem, especially in the last two sections. All the poetry that follows, including the "Four Quartets" is, in spite of many flashes of the old fire, moralistic poetry.

There is no strict law of evolution in a poet's work; there is not even a lawlessness in the evolution of a poet's work, for the creation of a poem is never an arbitrary event. For a time, for a year or perhaps five years, rarely more than ten, the divine madness descends on a mortal and then burns out. "The Hollow Men" is a celebration of this incineration. Mister Kurtz, he dead. A penny for the old guy. But Mr Kurtz, though he may have been a bad man, a corrupt man, a suffering man, saw visions that were splendid. Even when, as in this poem, he is evoking 'death's other kingdom', he does so in bright images, 'sunlight on a broken column', 'a tree swinging'; but then, alas, 'between the emotion/And the response/Falls the Shadow'. What Eliot meant by the Shadow is clear enough and it is not a Shadow that we encounter in his poetry without sorrow.

"Ash Wednesday" should be read with a poem of the same year, "Marina", where the new resolution is made clear in these lines:

> This form, this face, this life
> Living to live in a world of time beyond me; let me
> Resign my life for this life, my speech for that unspoken,
> The awakened, lips parted, the hope, the new ships.

The problem of poetry and belief was endlessly discussed in these years 1925–30, in print and in conversation. But though it was always posed as a problem of poetry and belief, what Eliot and Richards and the rest of us were discussing was poetry and beliefs— there is a difference between a belief which is a belief in God, or in the Incarnation, and the beliefs which are formulated as the Thirty-nine Articles or the Constitutions of the Society of Jesus. It is perhaps the same kind of distinction that Eliot himself made between philosophical belief and poetic assent, and I am only suggesting (following Kierkegaard) that we must distinguish between Christianity and Christendom. Eliot wrote (in his essay on Dante) that the advantage of a coherent traditional system of dogma and morals was that 'it stands apart, for understanding and assent *even without belief*, from the single individual who propounds it'. A man's faith is a reflection of his temperament or soul and as such need not conflict with the wayward gusts of poetic inspiration. In this it differs from those moral commands to which a man must, if he resigns his life and would have peace, assent. This was made clear by Pascal, and by Unamuno in *The Agony of Christianity*. The Jesuits did not ask for faith but for obedience; and that demand led Pascal, in a moment of agonized despair, to cry: *It will stultify you.* The fragmented conclusion of "The Hollow Men" is the same cry of despair:

> For Thine is
> Life is
> For Thine is the

Perhaps the key to Eliot's agony lies in his essay on Pascal; his was the same agony as Pascal's, but I think that in the end Eliot resigned his life for that life, *stultified his speech* for that unspoken law. Pascal, he said, was to be commended 'to those who doubt but who have the mind to conceive, and the sensibility to feel, the disorder, the futility, the meaninglessness, the mystery of life and suffering, and who can find peace through a satisfaction of the whole being'. Eliot himself, I believe, was not of those who doubt, but rather one of those great mystics who, in his own words, 'like St John of the Cross, are primarily for readers with a special determination of purpose.'

I do not presume to judge him; I even tremble as I attempt to reveal some of the dimensions of his agony. But if I am to give my first allegiance to poetry (and I do not for a moment question the allegiance that a Christian must give to one whom Kierkegaard called 'the unique person') it is not honest to pretend that the poet

can have any other life or kingdom but poetry. The Shadow that
falls between the emotion and the response is the shadow of the
moral law, the Tables of the Law, the Commandments. For a year
or two the old images will haunt the mind—

> Distraction, music of the flute, stops and steps of the mind
> over the third stair,
>
> Fading, fading . .

But eventually

> We must be still and still moving
> Into another intensity
> For a further union, a deeper communion.

'In my end is my beginning'—yes, but it is the end of the earthly
poet and the beginning of the redeemed sinner, 'the awakened, lips
parted, the hope, the new ships.' The old ships are left burning on
the waters

> Burning burning burning burning

VII

Carl Gustav Jung

(i)

In a sad letter I received shortly before his death on June 6, 1961, Jung complained of the misunderstanding that had been his lot. His fame was world-wide, but he confessed that he felt like Master Eckhart, who was entombed for six hundred years. 'I ask myself again and again, why there are no men in our epoch who could at least see what I am wrestling with. I think it is not mere vanity and desire for recognition on my part, but a genuine concern for my fellow beings. It is presumably the ancient functional relationship of the medicine man to his tribe, the "participation mystique" and the essence of the physician's ethos. I see the suffering of mankind in the individual's predicament and vice-versa.'

To describe himself as a medicine man is perhaps to play into the hands of those who were Jung's bitterest critics. In England especially the representatives of a tradition that claims to be empirical, positivist and common-sensical tended to dismiss Jung as a metaphysical idealist, a mystagogue, a man who began well as an associate of the rationalist Freud, but who then fell by the way-side, or rather, went up into the clouds. Jung's own protestations that he was first and foremost a scientist, recording what he observed, passed unheeded.

Psychology, to quote the definition preferred by William James (and Jung was the true successor of James) is 'the description and explanation of states of consciousness as such'. That is to say, it is

by definition a natural science whose objective phenomena range
from the first appearance of consciousness in animal life to the
subtlest manifestations in man's consciousness of a sense of the
numinous—his consciousness of what might lie beyond the range
of consciousness. The mystic's faith in a living God is just as much
a psychological fact as the homing instinct of a pigeon. The psychologist must be prepared to investigate the whole range of mental
phenomena, and it was Jung's distinction, as it had been James's,
to face such a task without fear or prejudice.

This comprehensiveness, a comprehensiveness far greater than
Freud's, was not only the distinctive mark of his genius, but also
the explanation of the scepticism with which his work was sometimes received in academic circles. But just as there are certain
distortions of history which we call historicism, or certain distortions of artistic style which we call mannerism, so there is a
distortion of science which we may call scientism; and it is so far
removed from the true spirit of science which, as Bacon said, takes
all knowledge to be its province, that it has become the real obscur-
antism of our time, turning a blind eye on all phenomena that
cannot be accommodated to its own myopic vision.

The world will dispute for many years the relative importance of
Freud and Jung, and may conclude in the end that their doctrines
are complementary. The two men at one period worked together,
travelled together and exchanged voluminous letters which, when
they are published, will be as significant as any literature of our
time. Jung often spoke of his association with Freud, with admiration and gratitude: but he knew Freud's weaknesses (he had analysed
him!) and he knew his own. He was a man of balanced judgement.

The difference between these two great psychologists was
fundamentally one of temperament, and a realization of this led
Jung to his investigation of psychological types—perhaps the most
fruitful aspect of his life's work. Freud was a fatalist—he could not
believe that man would ever subdue or sublimate his aggressive
instincts. Jung was not exactly an optimist, but he believed that if
only man would learn to listen to the intimations of his unconscious,

he might be saved. But this calls for many acts of humility, perhaps for a renunciation of pride that is scarcely conceivable.

Though Jung's belief in the role of the unconscious in the transformation of civilization earned him the doubtful titles of prophet and mystic, he himself always wished to be regarded as a medical psychologist. He chose, right at the beginning of his career, to work on the psychology and pathology of so-called occult phenomena, and this led him to the formulation of a 'depth psychology' that differs radically from the Freudian theory of psycho-analysis. From a layman's point of view it sometimes seems that the correspondences between the two points of view are more important than the differences, but only time can resolve the question.

To his basic training in medicine and experimental psychology, Jung added a vast reading in classical and modern literature, in philosophy and anthropology, in theology and mysticism. He had an easy command of Greek and Latin, and had collected many rare books in the pursuit of his arcane knowledge. A man of powerful build and commanding presence, he was at the same time courteous and cultivated, a fascinating talker, humorous, quizzical and engaging. It is often said that he retained something of the Swiss peasant in his make-up. I have seen him take an enormous clasp-knife from his pocket and unconcernedly peel an apple while he discussed some profound matter like the dogma of the Trinity. He was active and adventurous, genial and completely human. He won the devotion of all who came into close contact with him. The practical good he did in repairing broken lives and giving new hope to those in despair of themselves and the world can never be told in detail. It was on the basis of his unrivalled experience in human problems that he erected his philosophy of the unconscious. He did not believe that man could be saved by external means, social or political: each individual must come to terms with the dark forces within his own soul. Only to the degree that we each reconstitute the divided self can we hope to transform the world.

Jung was a great humanist—certainly the greatest that it has been my privilege to know. He was much misunderstood and sometimes bitterly criticized. This was because he believed that a doctor today cannot afford to withdraw to the peaceful island of undisturbed scientific work, but must descend into the arena of world events, in order to join in the conflicting battle of passions and opinions. Jung's work is controversial because it has a direct and disturbing bearing on world problems, which he knew to be essentially psychological problems.

As a medical psychologist he was convinced (and did not merely assume) that *nil humanum a me alienum esse* expressed a duty. In this belief he did not hesitate (again to the distress of academic critics) to apply his scientific methods to the analysis of social problems. Though he remained convinced that the individual must find his own salvation, he held that we are all children of one another, and carry within us as part of our psychic constitution the traces of collective experiences. This is, of course, one of the most disputed of his hypotheses, but in pursuit of its proof Jung did not hesitate to draw his evidence, not only from history, but even more effectively from contemporary events. Though he would have disclaimed the title of prophet, no writer of our time has traced with such accumulative accuracy the psychic origins of the social conflicts that have made the history of our time so tragic.

The range of his published work extends from treatises that are so clinical that they are beyond the comprehension of the layman to works that touch us all by their simplicity and humanity. It is sometimes said that Jung is an obscure writer. I do not agree. He is a writer with a personal style, and some of his expressions may have a rude vigour not suited to the academic medium; but in translation the writing is singularly clear and persuasive, quite devoid of rhetoric but occasionally rising to true eloquence.

My own approach to Jung's work has not been that of a professional psychologist, but that of a critic and philosopher of art and literature for whom psychology has been an indispensable instrument. There are many psychologists besides Jung to whom I have been indebted, but deep as my debt to any one of these may be, Jung stands in a special position of esteem simply because his knowledge of the material is so immense—far in excess of all other psychologists. It is true that in this particular field of the arts one did eventually reach a blind spot, and of this he was aware. During the last months of his life he had turned to the problem of contemporary art. He had in the past written essays on Joyce and Proust, and he now returned to what he regarded as the symptomatic problem of an 'alienated' art. 'The great problem of our time'—to quote again from his last letter to me—'is the fact that we don't understand what is happening in the world. We are confronted with the darkness of our soul, the Unconscious. It sends up its dark and unrecognizable urges . . . We are still in a shockingly primitive state of mind, and the main reason is that we cannot become objective in physical matters'. Our artists in particular, he felt, 'have not yet learned to be objective with their own psyche, to distinguish between the thing that you do and the thing that happens to you'. We have to learn to listen to what the psyche spontaneously says to us—through the dream, through the work of art. What is necessary is to attend to such intimations of the unconscious, with humility and submission.

We cannot separate a consideration of the quality of Jung's personality from our estimate of his scientific achievement—that surely is the lesson of Jung's own belief in the integration of the personality. To know Jung was to know the truth of this doctrine (he was its embodiment) but in the future his work will be judged by more objective standards. I cannot see any other scientific work of our time that combines in such perfection a deep knowledge of the human soul with a premonitory sense of human destiny.

Jung had two homes, both on the shores of Lake Zurich. The official residence, near to the city, where he interviewed his patients and received his countless visitors from all over the world, was large and beautifully furnished, a solid bourgeois home. But several miles up the lake, away from the road, he built a retreat with his own hands, converting a ruined tower into a hermit's cell. It was there that I sometimes visited him and listened to his words of wisdom as the wavelets lapped over the pebbles on the lake's edge.

These words of wisdom always brought us eventually to the problem of 'self-knowledge', the problem that has pre-occupied every great philosopher since Socrates. Self-knowledge is a fundamental necessity not only for philosophy and psychology, but also for science and politics. As Michael Polanyi, a scientist turned philosopher, has shown in one of the most significant books of our time,* 'any attempt rigorously to eliminate our human perspective from our picture of the world must lead to absurdity.' That human perspective, according to Jung (and according to Freud) must extend to those depths of the mind of which we are not normally conscious. Only if we succeed in recognizing the latent powers of the unconscious, for good and for evil, can we succeed in any human endeavour. Jung called this necessary task of integration 'the process of individuation' and it is the only means of bringing peace of mind to the individual and, by a species of contagion, of affecting other people with the same degree of equanimity.

A reliance on such a possibility is an immense 'act of faith', and it is necessary to ask ourselves what in such a context do we mean by the word 'faith', and if such a faith differs from the usual kind of faith, which is religious faith. To answer these questions I shall leave Jung for the moment and rely on Tolstoy.

In *A Confession*, written in 1879 immediately after completing *Anna Karenina*, Tolstoy relates in simple and moving words, how he recovered 'faith'. By faith he meant an acceptance of an irrational explanation of existence—an answer to those questions that cannot be answered by the reason: Why do I exist? Why does the world exist? What is the meaning and purpose of life? 'Reasonable knowledge had brought me to acknowledge that life is senseless— my life had come to a halt and I wished to destroy myself. Looking around on the whole of mankind I saw that people live and declare that they know the meaning of life. I looked at myself. I had lived

* *Personal Knowledge: Towards a Post-Critical Philosophy.* London (Routledge & Kegan Paul), 1958.

as long as I knew a meaning of life. As to others so also to me faith had given a meaning to life and had made life possible.' He did not define such faith or identify it with any particular religion. Indeed, 'looking again at peoples of other lands, at my contemporaries and their predecessors, I saw the same thing. Where there is life there, since man began, faith had made life possible for him, and the chief outline of that faith is everywhere and always identical.'*

Tolstoy does not identify this faith with a belief in God. Indeed, he admits that faith 'is not the relation of man to God (one has first to define faith, and then God, and not define faith through God) . . . faith is a knowledge of the meaning of human life in consequence of which man does not destroy himself but lives. Faith is the strength of life. If a man lives he believes in something. If he did not believe that one must live for something, he would not live. If he does not see and recognize the illusory nature of the finite, he believes in the finite; if he understands the illusory nature of the finite, he must believe in the infinite. Without faith he cannot live.'

I cannot quarrel with this argument. The only alternative argument is the materialist one, which interprets life in terms of mechanism, of matter that has spontaneously developed the capacity to transform itself, to evolve, to expand and contract, to disintegrate and to unify. A materialist may go so far as to assert that the universe displays some uniform tendency—to the conservation of energy, for example, or to formal simplicity. But such assertions cannot explain why such tendencies should exist, or tell us whether they are finite or infinite in duration. The materialist can always be driven into a position of nescience, and has to content himself with such logical banalities as *cogito ergo sum*, I think therefore I exist. These are precisely the kind of rational paradoxes that Tolstoy found so unsatisfying. They may lead to logical structures of amazing and even beautiful complexity, but

* My quotations are from Aylmer Maude's translations of Tolstoy's works published by the Oxford University Press (The World's Classics).

they do not answer the existential questions: Why do I exist, why does the world exist, what is the meaning of life?

There may be more to be said for the materialist argument than I have indicated here, but this essay is based on the assumption that it is basically unsatisfying to mankind and always will be. I agree with Tolstoy that man cannot live without some kind of faith, and that faith of some more or less obscure kind is what makes it possible for the great majority of people to live—to continue to live in spite of all the suffering and injustice in the world, in spite of the inevitability of death.

Tolstoy dismissed one or two kinds of false faith—epicurean faith, for example, whose only purpose is to provide consolation during life. He also dismissed superstitious faith, but here he made a distinction between the sophisticated superstitions of theologians and the simple superstitions of the poor and illiterate. Theology again is a diversion, a make-believe; whereas the simple faith of the poor is a reality that has practical value, in that it enables these simple folk to live and to suffer and to approach death with tran-quillity, even with gladness.

The problem for Tolstoy, and it is my problem and the problem of all intellectuals, is how is it possible to have a simple, naïve faith of this kind?

Tolstoy's solution of this problem seems to me to be illogical and self-deceptive. He does not rely on a mystical solution, on 'a moment of vision', on a Pascalian 'wager' or a Kierkegaardian 'leap into the abyss'. He says he returned, *deliberately and consciously*, to the state of grace that he possessed in his childhood and youth. 'I returned to the belief in that Will which produced me, and desires something of me. I returned to the belief that the chief and only aim of life is to be better, i.e. to live in accord with that Will.'

Will (with a capital W) is a term he derived from Schopenhauer, who was satisfied, as a philosopher, to leave it as a mysterious life-force. But in the very same paragraph Tolstoy proceeds to identify this Will with God. 'I returned to the belief that I can find the expression of that Will in what humanity, in the distant past hidden from me, has produced for its guidance: that is to say, I returned to a belief in God, in moral perfection, and in a tradition transmitting the meaning of life.'

This is a very muddled and illogical transition—from 'Will' to 'belief in God', 'belief in moral perfection', and belief in 'a tradition transmitting the meaning of life' (which Tolstoy proceeds, equally illogically, to identify with one such tradition, that represented by Christianity).

Will is an abstraction—a disembodied force or energy. God is a symbol, representing perhaps the source of this energy, but usually associated with anthropomorphic imagery of a more or less precise kind. Tradition is still another concept, implying an organization or church to codify and hand down a set of doctrines which define God in a particular manner and interpret the meaning of a faith in God—in other words, an orthodoxy with its sacraments and rituals.

Tolstoy was, of course, aware of these distinctions, and in the end he rejected orthodoxy and all sacraments and rituals: he became a particular kind of Christian with his own individualistic interpretation of the teachings of Christ—in fact, he founded a new heresy, Tolstoyism, which had many adherents throughout the world. His faith in God, therefore, was his own interpretation of the Christian faith, more particularly in certain aspects of Christ's teachings, those concerned with love and non-resistance to evil.

It is not my intention to criticize Tolstoy's interpretation of the Christian faith: I merely wish to arrive at an understanding of what is involved in the 'act' (as it is called) of faith. But I must first point out that Tolstoy's solution of the problem was not successful, either for himself or for other people. Tolstoy's disciples quarrelled with each other and gradually disintegrated as a religious group. Tolstoy himself remained an extremely unhappy man, causing distress to himself, his family and his friends. He himself acknowledged his failure in a play, *Light Shines in Darkness*, which he began in the 'eighties and continued in 1900 and 1902. It was left unfinished when he died in 1910. In his notes for the fifth act which was never written the character who represents Tolstoy says finally: 'I am always in doubt whether I have done right. I have accomplished nothing. Boris has perished. Vasili Nikonoryich has recanted. I set an example of weakness. Evidently God does not wish me to be his servant. He has many other servants—and can accomplish his will without me, and he who realizes this is at peace.' He is then shot by the mother of Boris (a youth who has been 'corrupted' by his teaching) and 'dies rejoicing that the fraud of the Church has been exposed, and that he has understood the meaning of life'.

It is tempting to be cynical and to suggest that it is a pity Tolstoy did not 'understand the meaning of life' before he had caused so much unhappiness to himself and others, but the real fallacy lies in the supposition that an understanding of 'the meaning of life' is the solution of what I have called, for the sake of brevity, the existential problem. It is not possible to understand the meaning of life—such an understanding is something beyond the reach of human reason. Even if science succeeds in understanding the whole mechanism of the universe, its origin and the origin of life on our planet, it would still be without a clue to the *meaning* of all this mechanism. A meaning is revealed only if we can discover the purpose of whatever confronts us—why it exists, and what is its function. Even if we can give a plausible explanation of the origin of life,* we must still seek to justify suffering and pain, which should not be necessary in a perfectly functioning mechanism. It is the grit in the machine that awaits a convincing justification.

There are two possible attitudes to this paradox (more than two, perhaps, but I think they reduce to two if one discounts the symbolic language in which they are expressed). The Christian attitude, which is basically common to all transcendental religions, sees in suffering and pain a trial by endurance: man has to suffer to deserve salvation in another sphere of existence (Heaven,

* Such as that given by Professor J. D. Bernal in *The Origin of Life*, London (Weidenfeld and Nicolson), 1967.

Nirvana). The other attitude is the Stoical one. It accepts suffering and pain (and man's inhumanity to man) as also inflictions to be endured, but endured without any hope of reward. In Greek tragedy there is the idea of retribution, the belief that the sufferings inflicted on man are due to his past follies, or the follies of his ancestors. The spectacle of such inevitable retribution should purge us of the false feelings that lead to acts of folly. We cannot escape suffering, but we can be conditioned to a calm acceptance of its inevitability.

This attitude I have called Stoicism, but I am perhaps giving a special meaning to the word. The original school of philosophers founded by Zeno in the fourth century B.C. taught that happiness, or serenity of mind, is to be attained by self-knowledge, by the mastering of the emotions and passions that otherwise disturb the 'even tenor' of our lives and lead to acts of folly. A similar philosophy had already been expounded in China by Laotze in the seventh century B.C., by Confucius in the sixth century, and by Chuang-tzu in the third and fourth centuries. These teachings are embodied in the Four Books—the Confucian Analects, the Great Learning, the Doctrine of the Mean, and the Works of Mencius. In spite of differences of detail and emphasis, there is common to all these Far Eastern philosophies a doctrine of the mean—of measure, of submitting the emotions and passions to an objective discipline or harmony. The Stoics are the Western representatives of this attitude, and there can be little doubt that they had access to the wisdom of the East.

Laotze was a contemporary of Buddha, and in its purest form Buddhism is again a philosophy of self-knowledge, of the attainment by discipline of serenity. But earlier than Buddha we have the Upanishads, and in the *Bhagavad Gita*, more than five thousand years ago, we find the same doctrine, that serenity of the mind is to be attained only by means of self-knowledge, 'Guided always by pure reason, bravely restraining himself, renouncing the objects of sense, and giving up attachment and hatred: enjoying solitude, abstemious, his body, mind and speech under perfect control, absorbed in meditation, he becomes free—always filled with the spirit of renunciation.'*

I do not wish to disguise the fact that all these philosophies and religions have symbols and rituals, terminologies and practices, which have little bearing on the problem we are discussing, but central to all of them is this doctrine of self-knowledge, of the attainment of serenity (and enlightenment) by the mastering and harmonizing of passions and desires.

All this is perhaps well-known, but there is now, especially among young people, a universal tendency to reject the very idea that a certain 'truth' exists, which we discover by renouncing the world and all human passions and desires, by submitting passively to evil and injustice, by meditation and prayer, or finally by the gift of grace. Truth, it is realized, is either an abstraction that we interpret with our own feeble faculties, or it is translated on our behalf into commandments or dogmas by a priesthood. Truth is something which we 'believe', that is to say, accept without rational proof. (Science does not claim to discover 'truth', but only certain degrees of probability. Or as Bertrand Russell says, ' . . . a belief is true when there is a corresponding fact, and is false when there is no corresponding fact'. But a belief in such correspondences is also fundamentally an act of faith, a 'commitment'.†) It is this search for truth, more specifically *a* truth, that is so delusive. The alternative process is the great tradition that stems from the *Gita*, the process of self-discipline, self-discovery, of what Jung calls the process of individuation, the coming-to-terms with the ambiguous Self. Unless one attains to this knowledge of the Self and thereby achieves inner (psychic) harmony, all our actions, however well-meaning, are self-defeating. Tolstoy never acquired this inner harmony; he remained a divided, frustrated and unhappy man, and inevitably communicated his disharmony to the world around him.

* The *Geeta*. The Gospel of the Lord Shri-Krishna. Trans. from the original Sanskrit by Shri Purohit Swami. London (Faber & Faber) 1935, p. 92.

† Cf. Michael Polyani, *Op. cit.*, *passim*, but especially chapter 10, 'Commitment'.

The word 'truth' may sometimes be used in translations of the *Gita* or the Four Books, but all modes of self-realization, of individuation, are essentially personal and pragmatic. Jung has given a modern psychological ('scientific') formulation to the same pragmatic process. Jung himself was fully aware that he was reformulating a science of sciences, a philosophy of being, that had its origins in remote antiquity.

It is perhaps not necessary to accept the hypothesis of the unconscious as expounded in such detail by Freud and Jung and other modern psychologists. One can substitute concepts such as the Devil, Original Sin, the Cosmic Vision, or some theory of conditional reflexes. What must be accepted, and is accepted in all religions from remotest antiquity, is the distinction between good and evil impulses or, in Marxist philosophy, between social integration and individual alienation. The desire and aim is always to heal this rift in man and society, and to establish the ideal of *mens sana in corpore sano*, where 'corpore' may refer to the human body or the body politic.

All these considerations lead to the question of 'wholeness'. In one of his earliest definitions of the process of individuation Jung says: 'Conscious and unconscious do not make a whole when one of them is suppressed and injured by the other. If they must contend, let it at least be a fair fight with equal rights on both sides. Both are aspects of life. Consciousness should defend its reason and protect itself, and the chaotic life of the unconscious should be given the chance of having its way too—as much of it as we can stand. This means open conflict and open collaboration at once. That, evidently, is the way human life should be. It is the old game of hammer and anvil, between them the patient iron is forged into an indestructible whole, an "individual".'*

The achievement of wholeness is beset with difficulties, mostly of our own creation or the creation of the society we live in. Its

* C. J. Jung, *Collected Works*, Vol. 9, Part I. *The Archetypes and the Collective Unconscious*, New York (Bollingen Series and London (Routledge & Kegan Paul) 1959. § 522.

achievement should be the purpose of education, but education as it is conducted in the modern world has generally the opposite effect, reinforcing all the maladjustments that inevitably arise in family life in a modern community. Because parents and teachers in general have so little understanding of psychology, we must have recourse to the psychiatrist. But a sane education could at least prevent the development of a psychosis in the child—the unhappy fate of millions of people in modern society. Since the seeds of this condition have been sown in the child's earliest years, he has acquired at home an attitude that unfits him for the collective life of the school and later for the collective life of society at large. Jung admits that 'it is quite outside the teacher's province to change the home atmosphere, although a little good advice can often work wonders even with parents. As a rule, however, the trouble has to be cured in the child himself, and this means finding the right approach to his peculiar psychology so as to render it amenable to influence . . . The first requisite is thorough knowledge of the home life. We know a great deal when we have found out the causes of a symptom, but still more is needed. The next thing we need to know is what sort of effects the external causes have produced in the child's psyche. This knowledge we obtain from a thorough investigation of his psychological life-history on the basis of his own and his parent's statements. Under certain conditions a good deal can be accomplished with just this information. Skilful teachers have applied this method all along . . . '*

And then Jung comes to the essential stage in the process of individuation:

'If we realize that the child gradually develops out of the unconscious state into a conscious one, we can understand why practically all environmental influences, or at any rate the most elementary and the most lasting of them, are unconscious. The first impressions of life are the strongest and most profound, even though they are unconscious—perhaps indeed for that very reason, for so long as they are unconscious they are not subject to change. We can only

* *Ibid.*, § 259.

correct what is in our consciousness; what is unconscious remains unchanged. Consequently, if we wish to produce a change we must first raise these unconscious contents to consciousness, so as to submit them to correction.'*

For various reasons Jung came to the conclusion that this difficult operation could not be undertaken in childhood. What is usually meant by an integrated personality—a well-rounded psychic whole that is capable of resistance and abounding in energy—is an *adult ideal*:

'No one can train the personality unless he has it in himself. And it is not the child, but only the adult who can achieve personality as the fruit of a full life directed to this end. The achievement of personality means nothing less than the optimum development of the whole individual human being. It is impossible to foresee the endless variety of conditions that have to be achieved. A whole lifetime, in all its biological, social, and spiritual aspects, is needed. Personality is the supreme realization of the innate idiosyncrasy of a human being. It is an act of high courage flung in the face of life, the absolute affirmation of all that constitutes the individual, the most successful adaption to the universal conditions of existence coupled with the greatest possible freedom for self-determination.'†

The difficulty, and even the danger, of this process is not ignored by Jung—is not this the way to develop monsters of egotism and tyranny? Nietzsche envisaged a superman of this sort, and in spite of all his qualifications, the result was a Mussolini or a Hitler. Jung's provision against such a development leads us back to faith—to what he first calls 'fidelity to the law of one's being', and then, since he must define this law, he describes it as 'an attitude such as a religious man should have towards God'. He does not, in this context, define God. He does, however, return to the subject in other works, such as *Psychology and Religion* and his autobiography, *Memories, Dreams, Reflections* (1963) which is essentially a description of how he himself achieved wholeness of personality.

Memories, Dreams, Reflections is in effect a confession, comparable

* *Ibid.*, § 260.   † *Ibid.*, § 289.

Carl Gustav Jung

to Tolstoy's *Confession*. I do not propose to summarize in a sentence or two a narrative of more than three-hundred pages, but there is one paragraph which I must quote because it describes an essential aspect of the process of individuation and one which fills many people with apprehension. Jung, some-time after the death of his wife, had a dream in which she appeared to him as a portrait. 'Her expression was neither joyful nor sad, but, rather, objectively wise and understanding, without the slightest emotional reaction, as though she were beyond the mist of affects.' Jung comments:

'The objectivity which I experienced in this dream and in the visions is part of a completed individuation. It signifies detachment from valuations and from what we call emotional ties. In general, emotional ties are very important to human beings. But they still contain projections, and it is essential to withdraw these projections in order to attain to oneself and to objectivity. Emotional relationships are relationships of desire, tainted by coercion and constraint; something is expected from the other person, and that makes him and ourselves unfree. Objective cognition lies hidden behind the attraction of the emotional relationship; it seems to be the central secret. Only through objective cognition is the real *conjunctio* possible.'*

It is the manifestation of such 'objective cognition' that leads to the appearance and charge of selfishness or egotism in all such methods of self-realization and individuation. The charge is made not only against Jung, but also against all those who practise various Oriental forms of Yôga. It has also been made against Gandhi. All such accusations are without foundation for the simple reason (embodied in the old saying: Physician, heal thyself) that a man who is divided against himself cannot effectively influence the fragmented psyches of other people. Tolstoy, as we have seen, is a typical example of such ineffectiveness. It is to be suspected that many psychiatrists fail for the same reason.

The problem of guidance is a real one, if only for the reason that

* *Memories, Dreams, Reflections.* Recorded and edited by Aniela Jaffé. Trans. by Richard & Clara Winston, London, 1963, p. 276.

137

teachers and psychiatrists do not exist in sufficient numbers to give direct instruction to the millions of alienated people that exist in the modern world. A technique of self-realization must be taught. But in general the individual, as Jung says, 'is so unconscious that he altogether fails to see his own potentialities for decision. Instead he is constantly and anxiously looking around for external rules and regulations which can guide him in his perplexity. Aside from general human inadequacy, a good deal of the blame for this rests with education, which promulgates the old generalizations and says nothing about the secrets of private experience . . . the individual who wishes to have an answer to the problem of evil, as it is posed today, has need, first and foremost, of *self-knowledge*, that is, the utmost knowledge of his own wholeness. He must know relentlessly how much good he can do, and what crimes he is capable of, and must beware of regarding the one as real and the other as illusion. Both are elements within his nature, and both are bound to come to light in him, should he wish—as he ought—to live without self-deception or self-delusion.'*

I believe that by constant self-examination and meditation the individual can attain self-knowledge. Naturally he will, and should, be influenced by teachers and psychiatrists, in so far as he comes into contact with them, and he can and should be influenced by the great teachers of the past, by Lao-tze and Buddha, by Christ and Mohammed, by Confucius and Plato, by Tolstoy and Gandhi, by Freud and Jung. Even if such teachers, as in the case of Tolstoy, never attained perfect self-knowledge, their struggle and their failure are of immense significance. But the individual must also be on guard against a mental confusion that may come about by listening to many different teachers. Maybe there are exceptional people who have exceptional insight into the methods that have been evolved by other cultures and other traditions, such as the Yôga of the East. These have been evolved for races whose minds have been formed by an entirely different environment and an entirely different method of upbringing. Jung, while paying tribute

* *Ibid.*, pp. 304–5.

to Yôga as a spiritual achievement as great as any the human mind has ever created, warns us that Yôga is not suitable for the peoples of the West. 'The spiritual development of the West has been along entirely different lines from that of the East and has therefore produced conditions which are the most unfavourable soil one can think of for the application of Yôga. Western civilization is scarcely a thousand years old and must first of all free itself from its barbarous one-sidedness. This means, above all, deeper insight into the nature of man. But no insight is gained by repressing and controlling the unconscious, and least of all by imitating methods which have grown up under totally different psychological conditions. In the course of the centuries the West will produce its own Yôga, and it will be on the basis laid down by Christianity.'*

What Jung meant by the basis laid down by Christianity is the same that Tolstoy meant, the same that Gandhi meant, that 'God is love'. Jung ends his autobiography with a meditation on this mystery,

'In my medical experience as well as in my own life I have again and again been faced with the mystery of love, and have never been able to explain what it is . . . we are in the deepest sense the victims and the instruments of cosmogonic "love". I put the word in quotation marks to indicate that I do not use it in its connotations of desiring, preferring, favouring, wishing, and similar feelings, but as something superior to the individual, a unified and undivided whole. Being a part, man cannot grasp the whole . . . Man can try to name love, showering upon it all the names at his command, and still he will involve himself in endless self-deception. If he possesses a grain of wisdom, he will lay down his arms and name the unknown by the more unknown *ignotum per ignotius*—that is, by the name of God.'

This, then, is the irreducible meaning of the word faith, of that faith in the meaningfulness of life and, as Tolstoy said, in consequence of which man does not destroy himself but lives. But we

---

* *Collected Works*, Vol. II, *Psychology and Religion: East and West*, § 876.

deceive ourselves (and others) if we are content with a passive acceptance of the meaningfulness of life, for what then is the difference between the meaningful and the meaningless? It does not suffice to admit our ignorance and fill the gap with the word God. Life has to be lived, and we are therefore driven back to the necessity of personal integration, which is a coming to terms with life as an organic experience, as a practical accommodation of all its aspects, known and unknown, conscious and unconscious. Without faith we cannot live, said Tolstoy. But equally we cannot live unless we come to terms with ourselves and our immediate social environment. There is nothing 'cosmogonic' about such an accommodation: it is a private and a human experience. It does not entitle us to speak about God; it does not demand that we should accept a creed or become members of a church. But it does assume that we enter into dialogue with our fellow human beings, establish open relationships 'between man and man', work and play with one another, love our neighbours as ourselves. These are ethical commonplaces, but they are rarely practised, or rarely successful, and this because they are attempted between individuals who have not accomplished the first necessity, which is to be at peace with themselves, which means to come to terms with the dark side of their own natures. Everything depends on this basic personal achievement. 'From the Son of Heaven down to the mass of people', it is said in *The Great Learning*, 'all must consider the cultivation of the person the root of *everything besides*.' The oldest wisdom in the world insists on this first necessity; the latest science of the psyche insists on the same first necessity. 'Spirituality implies equanimity.'

VIII

The Early Influence of Bertrand Russell

The most honest tribute one can make to a philosopher is to acknowledge as exactly as possible one's own permanent debt to him. But it is easier to acknowledge a debt than to come to a final settlement. In my own case the phase of absorption was relatively short but very intense. It began with *The Problems of Philosophy*, the little volume that was published in 1910, which I bought at the age of 19 at a time when I was devouring Nietzsche and other mental excitements indiscriminately. Its severely logical approach to a limited number of philosophical problems had a disciplinary effect and sent me to Hume and Kant for a historical grounding. I was too busy with other studies in the years immediately preceding the outbreak of the 1914 war, and with more extravert activities during the war, to have much opportunity to develop my natural liking for philosophy, but I bought and read *Principles of Social Reconstruction* as soon as it appeared in 1916, and towards the end or immediately after the war I acquired and read in quick succession, and in this order, *Mysticism and Logic*, *Roads to Freedom*, and *Our Knowledge of the External World*. Then in May and June, 1920, I attended a course of eight lectures given by Russell held in Dr Williams' Library, London—it was the first and only direct tuition in the subject I ever received, and the experience still remains vivid. These lectures were afterwards published as *The Analysis of Mind* (1921), and were followed six years later by the companion volume on *The Analysis of Matter*. There, I regret to say, either my devotion or my understanding expired.

The Early Influence of Bertrand Russell

But I had gathered an immense amount of insight from these seven volumes. I use the word 'insight' because it was a word used by Russell with a particular meaning that appealed to me then and has remained effective in my thought. It was, I now suppose, an acceptable substitute for the word 'intuition', which I was told was a dirty word in philosophical circles. At the same time as I was reading Russell I was also reading Bergson, and for some time these two philosophers were to play a game of see-saw in my mind. If in the end Bergson triumphed if only temporarily—it was not for lack of heeding the warnings of Russell. But when Russell observed that intuition 'seems on the whole to diminish as civilization increases', I was inclined to answer 'all the worse for civilization'. I might agree that 'direct acquaintance' with things is given fully in sensation, and does not require any special faculty for its apprehension. But I was already seeking for a definition of the kind of 'direct acquaintance' embodied in the work of art, and 'intellect' did not seem to describe it. Curiously enough it was Russell's account of mathematics, a subject outside my comprehension, which seemed to offer the right kind of analogy, and I underlined with enthusiasm the following passage in "The Study of Mathematics" (an essay in *Mysticism and Logic*):

'Against that kind of scepticism which abandons the pursuit of ideals because the road is arduous and the goal not certainly attainable, mathematics, within its own sphere, is a complete answer. Too often it is said that there is no absolute truth, but only opinion and private judgement; that each of us is conditioned, in his view of the world, by his own peculiarities, his own taste and bias; that there is no external kingdom of truth to which, by patience and discipline, we may at least obtain admittance, but only truth for me, for you, for every separate person. By this habit of mind one of the chief ends of human effort is denied, and the supreme virtue of candour, of fearless acknowledgement of what is, disappears from our moral vision. Of such scepticism mathematics is a perpetual reproof; for its edifice of truths stands unshakable and inexpugnable to all the weapons of doubting cynicism.'

Not that as a young man I was in any danger of succumbing to
this kind of scepticism. I had drank from the heady fountains of
Nietzsche and was seeking for confirmation of his doctrine of the
Superman! What Russell offered was not scepticism, but what he
called 'scientific method', and though the phrase was a little drastic,
as defined by Russell it offered me the necessary loophole into
aesthetics. In his essay on "Scientific Method in Philosophy",
which I read in 1920, 'insight' is given further significance as a
'first suggestion' of 'the most important truth'. 'Instinct, intuition,
or insight is what first leads to the beliefs which subsequently
reason confirms or confutes; but the confirmation, where it is
possible, consists, in the last analysis, of agreement with other
beliefs no less instinctive. Reason is a harmonizing, controlling
force rather than a creative one. Even in the most purely logical
realms, it is insight that first arrives at what is new.'

There was the concept I needed, and this was the sense I gave to
reason in my first book of literary criticism (1926), which I called
Reason and Romanticism with this definition in mind. It might just
as well have been called *Reason and Insight*, for insight is another
name for the creative faculty in the philosophy of romanticism.

Some marginalia I wrote into my copy of *Our Knowledge of the
External World* are perhaps of more interest as reflecting on the
limitations of my own philosophy at that time than as a valid
criticism of Russell's philosophy, but I will quote them because they
do illustrate the kind of stimulus that Russell gave to a younger
generation forty years ago:

Russell: 'If philosophy is to become scientific . . . it is necessary
first and foremost that philosophers should acquire the disinterested
intellectual curiosity which characterizes the genuine man of
science.' My comment: This is the fallacy of the 'scientific' school.
Once philosophy loses its humanistic relativity it becomes abstract
and unreal: limited, like mathematics. Knowledge for knowledge's
sake is as futile a doctrine as art for art's sake.

At the conclusion of the essay on "Scientific Method in Philosophy" I observed:

Scientific method can do no more than discover 'truth', i.e. true facts. But truth has value only when related to human life.

Conclusion: The scientific method is superior to the 'logical' and intuitive methods; but its results possess value only when related to human life: unrelated they become a mere abstract fantasy.

Philosophy is a prior synthetic activity of the mind. Ethics follows and is selective. The two activities should be regarded as inseparable and fallible in isolation.

But I found more to approve than to criticize throughout the volume, and I marked with especial emphasis a sentence towards the end which reads: 'These two processes, of doubting the familiar and imagining the unfamiliar, are correlative, and form the chief part of the mental training required for a philosopher'—a precept which I hope I have followed in all my intellectual activities.

The Analysis of Mind was first published in 1921, and I was rash enough to give it a long review in *The New Age* (September 1, 1921). I concentrated on whatever relevance the book might have for the psychology of the imagination, and welcomed what seemed to me to be a rational explanation of the process. I have never ventured to reprint this youthful essay, but I do so now because it shows the ground upon which I was subsequently to build my own aesthetic philosophy:

'The general implications of Mr Bertrand Russell's new book, "The Analysis of Mind", have already been noticed in *The New Age*, but there remain certain particular considerations of his theory relating to what might be called the psychology of inspiration, or of productive imagination, which justify a fresh reference. It will be remembered that Mr Russell's conclusion is, briefly, that "the ultimate data of psychology are only sensations and images, and their relations. Beliefs, desires, volitions, and so on, appear to be

144

complex phenomena consisting of sensations and images variously interrelated". With this analysis I think any writer (or any painter—but I will keep to my last) must agree; he may only doubt its adequacy. Mr Russell, of course, makes no pretension to analyse the particular phase of psychology we are concerned with; but he does incidentally cover most of the ground. The problem is even stated, implicitly, at the end of the chapter on Words and Meaning: "Those who have a relatively direct vision of facts are often incapable of translating their vision into words, while those who possess the words have usually lost the vision. It is partly for this reason that the highest philosophical capacity is so rare: it requires a combination of vision with abstract words which is hard to achieve, and too quickly lost in the few who have for a moment achieved it." This capacity for expressing direct vision in abstract words is the very definition of the artist, and the great philosopher is only rare because the great artist is rare: he is a species of that genus. But what exactly is this capacity?—how does it manifest itself and what is its machinery? Mr Russell's analysis does not give an answer.

'Elsewhere, in dealing with memory and mnemic causation, Mr Russell comes to the conclusion that in all probability these processes are reducible to ordinary physical causation in nervous tissue. The units in the processes are sensations and images, which are in their turn probably physical units. One phenomenon not noticed by Mr Russell, but which, speaking on the evidence of those who experience the spontaneous fusion of vision and words, seems to be in varying degrees an essential feature of the creative process, appears to offer distinct confirmation of the hypothesis of physical causation. When a writer is faced with a problem of expression (is urged, that is, to give form to some emotion, whether sensational or intellectual) he may at the moment of urgence be baffled, utterly dumb. If he is writing against time, or for one of Mr Squire's journals, he will, by aid of thesaurus and dictionary, force his unwilling mind to arrive at an approximation in abstract words of the vision to be expressed. But if he is wise he will merely wait; and in an indeterminate course of time the words come, exactly expressive of the thing seen. The only possible explanation of this fact is that the mind, given raw material, will work unconsciously to create. You place the unbaked dough into the oven and in course of time you find bread. Again, the only possible explanation of this explanation appears to me to be an hypothesis that the vision, or prevision, that urged the artist to expression, took physical shape in the nervous tissue of the brain: but that shape was too amorphous to be recognized by the ready counters (abstract words) *at that time* in physical association with the units of vision. But a centre of attraction had been established and in process of time that centre will attract the units of expression: the words that fit. And such, I think, is possibly the machinery that combines vision with abstract words, and determines, by its efficiency, the capacity of the philosopher—and of the artist.

'Lest readers should take this theory of inspiration as surely materialism running away with itself, I would draw attention to a further development of Mr Russell's analysis that quite decisively alters the complexion of the case—I mean the problem of truth and falsehood. The formal solution of this problem is not difficult: it consists in verifying propositions by relating their constituent images to the objectives meant. But this formal solution, as Mr Russell points out, though true, is inadequate. "It does not, for example, throw any light upon our preference for true beliefs rather than false ones. This preference is only explicable by taking account of the causal efficacy of beliefs, and of the greater appropriateness of the responses resulting from true beliefs. But appropriateness depends upon purpose, and purpose thus becomes a vital part of theory of knowledge." And, we may add, of theory of aesthetic. Art, in so far as it is expression, is a material process. Within the limits of this process much beauty, of "gem-like flame", may exist. But the beauty that is non-material—that is spiritual and thereby so definitely higher—derives its existence and nature from the existence and nature of a purpose. Whether the purpose is aesthetic in origin, or whether it is economic or ethical in character, perhaps doesn't really matter. But it does seem to me that beauty (which we might safely, because vaguely, say *is* the purpose of all art) is a quality of moral action, as well as of significant form: that beauty is dynamic as well as static: and this is the be-all and end-all of all confused theories about "pure" art, about art for its own sake, art "striving to be independent of the mere intelligence".

'There are obvious dangers in the extreme view on the relation of beauty to ethics, but when it is advanced firmly, though not narrowly, by so serious and so complete a critic as Professor Irving Babbitt, it would be well not to dismiss it too hurriedly. In his book, *Rousseau and Romanticism*—which, I am glad to see, is having a very vitalizing, and a continually increasing, influence on our current literary standards—Professor Babbitt can be as forthright as follows:

The attempt to divorce beauty from ethics led in the latter part of the eighteenth century to the rise of a nightmare subject— aesthetics . . . We would not hesitate to say that beauty loses most of its meaning when divorced from ethics even though every aesthete in the world should arise and denounce us as philistines. To rest beauty upon feeling, as the very name aesthetics implies, is to rest it upon what is ever shifting.

'To that statement with its appertaining arguments I see no answer. The only tenable opposition seems to be that typified by a modern school of art critics—I mean Mr Clive Bell and Mr Roger Fry. Their theory rests on the assumption of a separate aesthetic emotion, from the manifestations of which it is possible to deduce the science of aesthetics. Unfortunately, this emotion is peculiar to a narrow sect of people, mostly painters, and it is extremely difficult to establish causal laws of any universal applicability. But a science lacking universal laws is a misnomer; and for this reason, if for no other, we are driven to the same conclusion as Professor Babbitt: that aesthetics is a fiction of the romantic mind. And Croce notwithstanding; for his Aesthetic is not "the science of beauty", but the science of expression, and in this sense is more allied to what I have called the psychology of inspiration, or of productive imagination. If these conclusions are admitted, the consequences are rather alarming: it means that we must "scrap" all aesthetic philosophies that rest on a conception of art as a separate manifestation of the mind, and adopt, on the one hand, the analytical methods of Croce (and even those of Mr Russell) and, on the other hand, revert to the type of criticism represented by Lessing—the greatest of all critics since Aristotle: a criticism based on the intrinsic nature of the artist's craft. The separate spheres of philosophy, psychology and criticism cover all the necessary field of art; aesthetics can only be a confused mingling of these three.'

All this has very little to do with the main purpose of *The Analysis of Mind*, which was rather to show that a wrong philosophy of matter had caused many of the difficulties in the philosophy of mind, and that 'consciousness is a complex and far from universal characteristic of mental phenomena'. This led me straight to Freud and Jung, and if the consequent switch meant that I to a large extent abandoned philosophy for psychology, the fact is to be attributed largely to *The Analysis of Mind*.

By way of compensation I had already been drawn in another direction taken by Russell's own interests. *Principles of Social Reconstruction* was published in 1916, five years before *The Analysis of Mind;* and *Roads to Freedom* in 1918. I read both books immediately after their publication, while serving in the Army. I should explain that I was already calling myself an anarchist, and I read these two volumes for whatever support they might lend to my own political philosophy. I found a great deal, especially in *Roads to Freedom*, where Anarchism is indeed considered as one of the three possible 'roads', the others being socialism and syndicalism. As a matter of fact, I was equally interested in syndicalism, having been drawn by Orage into the Guild Socialist movement. Syndicalism, or Guild Socialism, I argued, was the practical application of anarchist principles to an industrial community. Russell gave a good deal of support to these ideals, always reverting, however, to the psychological realities. 'The supreme principle, both in politics and in private life', he asserted, '*should be to promote all that is creative, and so to diminish the impulses and desires that centre round possession.*' 'Production without possession, action without self-assertion, development without domination' was the epigraph (from Lao-Tzu) that he put on the title-page of *Roads to Freedom*. But what do these ideals amount to when translated into practical politics? In his Introduction to *Roads to Freedom* Russell considered and rejected Anarchism, Marxism, Socialism and Syndicalism and decided in favour of Guild Socialism (which he distinguished from Syndicalism): 'the best practical system', and he even conceded, on the last page of his book, that his conception of Guild Socialism leant 'more, perhaps towards Anarchism than the official Guildsman would wholly approve'. 'It is in the matters that politicians usually ignore—science and art, human relations, and the joy of life—that Anarchism is strongest . . . The world that we must seek is a world in which the creative spirit is alive, in which life is an adventure full of joy and hope, based rather upon the impulses to construct rather than upon the desire to retain what we possess or to seize what is possessed by others.' This, and much more, followed by the confident assertion that 'such a world is possible: it waits only for men to wish to create it', aroused my youthful enthusiasm; but then came the post-war years, the great disillusion with politicians and trade unionists, the gradual abandonment of hope and the growth of cynicism and despair. *Roads to Freedom* makes sad reading today. It is not that the roads led to nowhere: none of them was ever trodden; and I think Russell himself turned away from any faith in political action, concentrating on the slow piecemeal process of education, the principles of which he practised as well as preached. Someone once expressed the view that the best form of government is tyranny tempered with assassination; Russell would probably substitute democracy modified by direct action. But I hope that he still believes that pure Anarchism is the ultimate ideal.

I cannot make any cold assessment of Bertrand Russell's position as a philosopher—partly because I am not competent in this field and partly because I do not think that he is a philosopher of any assessable academic status. He has been essentially a teacher—a teacher in the sense that Socrates was a teacher, and he has had a great influence on the minds of at least three generations—his own, mine, and the generation that has just reached maturity. This influence, I believe, has been wholly for the good, not in any specifically ethical sense, but in the sense of the good life. He has vitalized thought at innumerable points and has always represented for me and I am sure for many others the embodiment of these Socratic virtues,—self-control, fairness, courage, liberality and sincerity— which are the characteristics of a mind free from anxiety and fear.

IX

Richard Aldington

I first met Richard Aldington on some occasion when we were both on leave from the Front—I think it must have been late in 1916 or early 1917. I had for some years admired him as a poet and had eagerly read everything that he wrote for *The Egoist*, *Poetry and Drama* and *The Little Review*. Groups of his poems had appeared in such anthologies as *Des Imagistes* (March, 1914), in *Some Imagist Poets* (1915) and *Some Imagist Poets 1916*—anthologies which he had helped to edit. The prefatory manifestoes in these anthologies became my own poetic creed and Aldington's first volume of poems, *Images (1910–1915)*, which was published by the Poetry Bookshop (price 8d net) with a coloured woodcut on its paper cover by John Nash, became one of my most treasured possessions—I still have it. I had looked forward to our meeting, therefore, with great eagerness and I was not disappointed. We immediately became friends and with intervals of silence due to war and exile, remained friends to the end. The last of many letters from him that have survived is dated 28/10/61—the first, written in pencil from his unit in France (inscribed 'Ex vinculis') predates it by forty-two years.

I well remember that first meeting. We had lunch together and then strolled up Charing Cross Road, looking at the bookshops and talking about our literary enthusiasms. Aldington looked very handsome in his uniform and I was immediately captivated by the brightness and candour of his features—a boyishness, one might call it, which he retained perhaps all his life, certainly until he left

Europe. He was one of the most stimulating friends I have ever had—easy in conversation and very frank, full of strange oaths (mostly in French), his mind darting about rapidly from one aspect of a subject to another. I was to spend many happy hours with him, at first in London and then, when he went to live at Malthouse Cottage, Padworth, on weekends which I spent there from time to time. It was a friendship not free from divergences of opinion—even fundamental differences of outlook, as I shall now try to explain.

After the war Aldington quickly re-established himself as an editor and reviewer. His main interest was French literature, of which he had a quite exceptional knowledge, but he was also a poet and with the publication of *Death of a Hero* in 1929, an outstanding novelist. But the progress from imagist poet of 1915 to the novelist of 1929 was not accomplished without some strain on his own character and on our friendship. The first fact to realize is that sometime between the publication of the second Imagist anthology (1916) and the end of the war Aldington had abandoned his imagist ideals. We find Ezra Pound, in a letter to Margaret Anderson in August, 1917, already predicting that Imagism was finished as a movement. 'I don't think any of these people have gone on; have invented much since the first *Des Imagistes* anthology.' Pound had reasons of his own for dismissing the Imagists—there had been quarrels mainly due to the inclusion of Amy Lowell in the group— Pound detested her and her work. But there is more direct evidence of Aldington's own change of heart and style in a letter dated 29/3/22 which is in my possession though it was not written to me— I think the 'mon cher' addressed in it must have been Harold Monro, and Monro must have passed it on to me since it gives a very careful and objective criticism of a collection of my own poems. These were subsequently published by the Hogarth Press (*Mutations of the Phoenix*, 1923), but I had perhaps first submitted them to the Poetry Bookshop.

'You will notice', Aldington writes, 'that the trend of the new school (as always) is to throw over its immediate predecessors. Thus our poetry was the poetry of the emotions and of beauty, of instinct and sudden impulse; it sought to share an "état d'âme"; its ideal of style was something clear, economical, exquisitely correct. Read (and others of his "school") try to create poetry from thought and the operations of the intelligence; psychology and character interest them; beauty is a phenomenon not a passion, they analyse love, they don't overflow with it. Instead of a jet of emotion immobilized by words into a silver fountain, they build a pillar of four dimensions cemented and rigid with intellect. Their style is allusive and elliptic; their vocabulary abstruse and ponderous; their meaning tenuous and remote. We limited our audience to those who feel intensely and delicately; they to those who think deeply and abundantly. We were sentimentalists; they are anatomists. We committed many follies, but they are wise; we were as silly as doves, but they as subtle as serpents. We secured a few hundred readers; they will have a few scores.'

Aldington concluded (after further interesting comparisons): 'I think he has done well in a genre I don't like. I commend him inasmuch as I am (or try to be) an impartial critic and I deplore him as a member of a rival sect'. I myself would not have thought of myself as a member of a rival sect, but as the letter elsewhere makes clear, the rival sect that Aldington had in mind was that of T. S. Eliot. There is no doubt that Aldington from this time onwards became highly suspicious of, if not antagonistic towards, the direction that English writing was taking under the tutelage of Eliot. In answer to some friendly criticism I had made of *A Fool i' the Forest*, the long poem Aldington published in 1924, he wrote:

'If the Fool strikes you as loose in structure, texture and idea, I reply that you call "loose" what I call ease, fluidity, clarity . . . Ten years, five years ago, I should have said Amen to your denunciation. Now, I take it as a compliment! I abandon, cast off, utterly deny the virtue of "extreme compression and essential significance of every word". I say that is the narrow path that leadeth to sterility. It makes a desert and you call it art. Pound, Flint, both went down on that; I saw them go; and I shall live to see you and Tom go the same way.' He then reveals his own new hopes: 'I think this and the next decades of our lives should be a period of intense production and widening audiences. God save me from the fate of Pound and save you too! I say, pox on your intensities and essences; know what you know, feel what you feel, think what you think, and put it down, write, write, write'.

The argument went on through several more letters, but they only served to make it clear that Aldington was now in full revolt against what he called the paradoxes and shibboleths of the intelligentsia. In a letter of 9/1/25 he writes: 'I am rebelling against a poetry which I think too self-conscious, too intellectual, too elliptic and alembiqué. This poetry is (selon moi) distinguished by over-elaboration of thought and expression and by a costiveness of production'. And in the same letter there is this revealing passage:

'I don't profess to know what Eliot's influence on me has been; I suspect that, like Pound's of old, it is rather negative than positive, warning me off, rather than luring me on. Like most English writers, I have found the one overwhelming influence to be Shakespeare. To escape it I fled to the French and to the Greeks, but to small avail. I find him in everything I write.'

His letters become increasingly bitter in this year, but at the same time defiant. 'I feel in a severely practical mood', he told me. 'In answer to the question: For whom am I writing? As many people as will read me. Hence the necessity for as much energy and clarity and essential simplicity as one can compass.' He began to write a series of articles for the newly established *Vogue*, and this led him to review 'the whole movement from 1908 to the present day'. I do not know whether the planned series of sixteen articles was ever completed, or has survived, but it would have been of great historical interest. Here is a paragraph from an undated letter of this time that throws some welcome light on the origins of the Imagist movement:

'I think it was a pity to drop that little sneer at the imagists but of course one must say what one honestly believes. I don't know what Pound got from Hulme, but I do know that my debt to Hulme = o. I disliked the man and still dislike him though he's dead. Also, I had written what Pound christened "imagist" poems before I had ever heard of Hulme. The point is that imagism, as written by H.D. and me, was purely our own invention and was not an attempt to put a theory in practice. The "school" was Ezra's invention. And the first imagist anthology was invented by him in order to claim us as his disciples, a manoeuvre we were too naïf to recognize at the time, being still young enough to trust our friends.'

There is another interesting confession in a letter of 2/7/25. He has been defending his use of the phrase 'innate art sense' as an essential basis of criticism and writes: 'By "innate art sense" I know I beg a dozen questions and probably write nonsense. But, as always, I here try to keep my eye on the fact. Now, between the ages of 15 and 16, the sight of Barfreston Church, a visit to the Musée Royale at Brussels, the discovery of English poetry, entirely changed my life. I recognized these things, without being told to do so, as a series of Columbus-like discoveries in my young life. My sister had exactly the same opportunities and remained entirely different. I conclude that I had an "innate art sense" and she hadn't'.

A great deal of correspondence that follows towards the end of 1925 and through 1926 concerns a project called "The Republic of Letters", a series of critical biographies he had undertaken to edit for Routledge. There was also to be a series of Broadway Translations, but the discussion of possible authors and impossible terms is perhaps not of general interest. There are some amusing letters about Voltaire, his own chosen author, and a refusal to discuss Dante (the Commedia an imposing desert with marvellous oases, but these unfortunately become less frequent as the work proceeds). He prefers Virgil.

In August, 1926, comes a sad and significant note: 'I am very, very tired, more tired than I have ever been in my life and wondering if I am going to collapse. In fact, I feel damned ill'. He went to Italy for a holiday and by the end of the year he was himself again, and accusing me of sounding a little weary—'overwork, my boy. The mind doesn't get tired, but the nerves or something physical connected with thinking and writing do'. He says in the same letter, 'We saw a good deal of Lawrence in Italy—cantankerous and amusing as ever. He is hideously narrow-minded and too self-centred. But I like him very much, he is someone. He had a bug about founding an independent review, etc. I told him I thought independent reviews were bunk, and that for my part I can say all I have to say in reviews already established, that I see no point in writing for a few hundred people when you can say exactly the same thing to a good many thousand. So he revenged himself by saying I had no experience of the world'.

For some time now Aldington's thoughts had been turning to the possibility of writing a novel with his war experience as a background. On 15/7/29 he writes:

'I am sending you under another cover the proofs of 384 pages of my novel, and will forward the remainder as soon as they arrive. The proofs are for you alone—you know it's bad for a book to get about too much before publication. The English edition has been mutilated by the publishers, and I am trying to insist on the substitution of asterisks. In some places they have cut a whole page! God knows why, for it's pretty harmless. If you can spare time to read the novel, I'd like your comments, particularly on the war portions. At the point these proofs break off, there are still nearly 50 pages of war stuff to come. I hope you won't wholly disapprove— I always remember your saying that we should not allow ourselves to be cheated of a great experience by the attitude of the pacifists who weren't in it. Anyhow, I've purged my bosom of perilous stuff, and look forward to more creative work.'

He adds: 'I don't expect my novel to be treated with candour or fairness in England, but since I am making good rapidly in America, it leaves me more or less indifferent. However, I think you'll admit they'll have to take some notice of the novel. I suppose they'll say I imitated Remarque (excellent book!) but I didn't read him until my own book was in type'.

The enormous success of *All Quiet on the Western Front* had, however, prepared the public for *Death of a Hero* and Aldington sailed to fame and freedom on this new wave of 'war books'. He was never to be quite the same friend so far as I was concerned— not that his affection ever diminished, or that he grew distant and conceited, but I have experienced in other cases the desolation that fame brings to friendship. We continued to exchange letters through 1930 and 1931, and there is much interesting discussion of the writing of the novels and short stories that followed *Death of a Hero*. There are no letters from 1932, but the correspondence revives again in 1933 suddenly to cease, for no apparent reason, with a letter written on the last day of 1934. Characteristically, it was a letter concerned about my own welfare—I was in temporary diffi- culties and Aldington, always kind and considerate to his friends, was trying to find me work with a London publisher.

I suspect that some letters must have been lost, for the next is dated more than eleven years later and came from Hollywood. It is a reply to one I had written from France, where I must have been on some official mission, and describes in mock-modest terms his new life in America. 'I'm not much good at present—my salary is only $1,000 a week—but I have a kind of obstinate hankering to master this infernal trade at which nearly all English writers fail.' I had asked him to come back to Europe and help in the work of cultural reconstruction after the war. 'Your suggestion that I should return to Europe is rather like telling someone who, by dint of forethought and at some expense, has got a Pullman seat in a train de luxe to come and frolic in an Hommes 40 Chevaux 8. Merci, mon prince!' But the train de luxe did not get him anywhere. Eighteen months later he is writing: 'These people degenerate on acquaintance . . . It is partly a difference of our temperaments, but partly also the result of residence, that I long ago ceased to expect any real contact or friendship with Americans, and lived with the landscape, the still extensive relics of primitive America. Rather as Lawrence did—except that I think his red Indians detestable and boring barbarians . . . I find myself hankering after France, but I am afraid of cold and food deficiencies for the child. What do you advise?'

There is something pathetic about that question, and I no longer remember how I answered it. But as we know, he did eventually return to France, to live and work in comparative modesty for the few years that were left to him. France was always, I believe, his 'spiritual home', and I think he was perhaps happier there than he had ever been in England or California.

I met him once or twice on his rare visits to London—the same gay but caustic Richard that I had first met in London forty years earlier. He urged me to come and visit him in Montpellier, but I was never able to go. His last letter was on the occasion of H.D.'s death, thanking me for the brief obituary I wrote for *The Times*. He was sad and disillusioned, talked of his old friends, Unkil Ez and Wyndham (Lewis), and described his new public in the U.S.S.R. 'Personally, I think it an error to bother with the highbruffs . . . One should hope to reach the quiet "reading man" and this new proletarian "public" which will buy practically anything the booksellers shove at it'.

That is sad. I prefer to think that Richard Aldington will be remembered by his 'images'—images of war and of love. "After Two Years" is perhaps not specifically 'imagist', but it is one of the most perfect lyrics in the English language.

> She is all so slight
> And tender and white
> As a May morning.
> She walks without hood
> At even. It is good
> To hear her sing.
>
> It is God's will
> That I love her still
> As he loves Mary.
> And night and day
> I will go forth to pray
> That she love me.

Richard Aldington

She is as gold
Lovely, and far more cold.
  Do thou pray with me,
For if I win grace
To kiss twice her face
  God has done well to me.

Imagism was too limited in its ideals to survive as a poetic
'movement', but it was a necessary stage in the evolution of English
poetry, and Aldington, H.D., and Flint purified the literary atmosphere between 1910 and 1915 and prepared the way for the emer-
gence of greater poets like Pound and Eliot. Perhaps the "Proem"
which Aldington wrote in May, 1917, and placed at the beginning
of his *Images of War* has some prophetic reference to his own
career:

  Out of this turmoil and passion,
  This implacable contest,
  This vast sea of effort,
  I would gather something of repose,
  Some intuition of the inalterable gods.

  Each day I grow more restless,
  See the austere shape elude me,
  Gaze impotently upon a thousand miseries
  And still am dumb.

Aldington did not remain 'dumb', but his novels belong to the
turmoil and passion of this age, and I prefer to think that he did, in
his poetry, gather something of repose, some intuition of the
inalterable gods.

X

D. H. Lawrence

Walter Bagehot described Charles Dickens as 'an irregular genius', but the cap fits D. H. Lawrence. 'D. H. Lawrence *was* a genius', asserts Richard Aldington in his biography,* but asks: 'what sort of a genius?' Bagehot provides him with an answer—page after page of his brilliant essay could be quoted and with the substitution of the name, would apply perfectly to Lawrence. Let us try the experiment:

The truth is, that Lawrence wholly wants the two elements which we have spoken of as one or other requisite for a symmetrical genius. He is utterly deficient in the faculty of reasoning. 'Mamma, what shall I think about?' said the little girl. 'My dear, don't think', was the old fashioned reply. We do not allege that in the strict theory of education this was a correct reply; modern writers think otherwise; but we wish someone would say it to Mr Lawrence. He is often troubled with the idea that he must reflect, and his reflections are perhaps the worst reading in the world. There is a sentimental confusion about them; we never find the consecutive precision of mature theory, or the cold distinctness of clear thought. Vivid facts stand out in his imagination; and a fresh illustrative style brings them home to the imagination of his readers; but his continuous philosophy utterly fails in the attempt to harmonize them— to educe a theory or elaborate a precept from them . . . his didactic humour is very unfortunate: no writer is less fitted for an excursion to the imperative mood . . . his abstract understanding is so far

* *Portrait of a Genius, But* . . . London (Heinemann), 1950.

inferior to his picturesque imagination as to give even to his best works the sense of jar and incompleteness, and to deprive them altogether of the crystalline finish which is characteristic of the clear and cultural understanding.

Personally I would question one detail in the application of such an indictment to Lawrence—his failure to educe a theory or elaborate a precept from his extreme sensibility to circumstances—but Aldington would not have objected. 'Those who go to Lawrence for a coherent philosophical system', he tells us, 'or require him to state reasons and draw maps for everything he said or wrote, waste their time. What matters is not his opinions and prejudices, but himself, the life and beauty he can transmit more than anyone else of his age. As to contradiction, who does not contradict himself unless he happens to be unusually dull or a repulsively canny and crafty careerist?'

Twenty-five years ago Edwin Muir wrote a criticism of Lawrence which was substantially the same as Bagehot's criticism of Dickens. A copy of the review reached Lawrence and we have his reaction to it in a scornful article called "Accumulated Mail" which is reprinted in the Penguin *Selected Essays*. He lists nine points from Muir's review, rather with the intention of showing up their niggling irrelevance than with any idea of answering them. 'For me,' he concludes, 'give me a little splendour, and I'll leave perfection to the small fry.'

A little splendour—he meant the occasional and fugitive splendour of the rainbow, an image he uses in this same article. Lawrence found a little splendour and caught it in a net of words—no sensitive critic will deny that. But a question persists and again Bagehot will express it for us: though Muir expressed it too. 'He has not submitted himself to any discipline', he wrote. To which Lawrence retorted that 'the little god in a Ford machine cannot get at the thing worth having, not even with the most praiseworthy little engine of a will'. But Bagehot is more explicit, and just as concerned as Lawrence for 'the thing worth having'. He has been discussing the submission to discipline observable in men of regular and symmetrical genius and continues:

But the case is very different with men of irregular or anomalous genius, whose excellencies consist in the *aggravation* of some special faculty, or at the most of one or two. The discipline which will fit him for the production of great literary works is that which will most develop the peculiar powers in which he excels; the rest of the mind will be far less important, it will not be likely that the culture which is adapted to promote this special development will also be that which is most fitted for expanding the powers of common men in common directions. The precise problem is to develop the powers of a strange man in a strange direction.

That, it seems to me, was Lawrence's problem. He was a strange man and he had peculiar powers. Did he develop those powers in the most effective way, or was he led astray by incompatible ambitions?

It is easy to get on a high horse and gallop over the poor devil who is down and out. I have no desire to do that in the case of Lawrence—he has been too near to me in age and origins, in ideals and aspirations. At the age of seventeen or eighteen I discovered his first poem in *The English Review*. I bought *The White Peacock* as soon as it appeared, and I had *The Rainbow* on order from the publisher before it appeared, so that I got my copy before the first edition was seized by the police. I was a young subaltern then, and I remember writing a gauche letter of sympathy to the persecuted author, no doubt an unexpected and even unwelcome tribute from such a quarter. Lawrence was a hero to me and though I never met him, I was one of the first to visit his grave in Vence. Such personal details are relevant because they show that whatever other powers Lawrence may have lacked, he had the capacity to rouse the enthusiasm and inspire the minds of his contemporaries.

Richard Aldington played down this side of Lawrence too much: he himself was anti-intellectualist, scornful of 'that quasi-philosophising which now passes as criticism'. Works of Lawrence such as *Psychoanalysis and the Unconscious* and *Fantasia of the Unconscious* are barely mentioned and do not appear in the bibliography at the end of his volume. But Lawrence was first and foremost what Aldington calls a quasi-philosopher. *First and foremost*—for he asserted his Foreword to the *Fantasia*, that it seemed to him 'that even art is utterly dependent on philosophy: or if you prefer it, on a metaphysic. The metaphysics or philosophy may not be anywhere very accurately stated and may be quite unconscious, in the artist, yet it is a metaphysic that governs men at the time, and is by all men more or less comprehended and lived. Men live and see according to some gradually developing and gradually withering vision. That vision exists also as a dynamic idea or metaphysics— exists first as such. Then it is unfolded into life and art.' He went so far as to assert that 'this pseudo-philosophy of mine—"polly-analytics", as one of my respected critics might say—is deduced from the novels and poems, not the reverse. The novels and poems come unwatched out of one's pen. And then the absolute need which one has for some sort of satisfactory mental attitude towards oneself and things in general makes one try to abstract some definite conclusions from one's experiences as a writer and as a man. The novels and poems are pure passionate experience. These "polly-analytics" are inferences made afterwards, from the experience.'

Presumably Aldington did not feel this same 'absolute need', for his whole book is a denial of this side of Lawrence—a betrayal, not an examination and consequent rejection. The real importance of Lawrence, in my opinion, lies in his awareness of the 'withering vision' of our modern world, and in his determination 'to rip the old veil of a vision across, and find what the heart really believes in, after all: and what the heart really wants, for the next future. And we've got to put it down in terms of belief and of knowledge. And then go forward again, to the fulfilment in life and art.' An artist like Lawrence is not driven to science and metaphysics and 'polly-analytics' out of perversity—or, as Aldington, himself indulging momentarily in pollyanalytics, ventures to suggest, out of a power complex. 'Was it not Lawrence's worst error in life', he writes, 'to think that because he had unique and very real power as an artist and a personality he was also entitled to the very different power of the man of action, the ruler, the messiah? Certainly the hope haunted him for years, and the inevitable frustration maddened and embittered him.' This is to miss the point by an astronomical distance, and the gloss that follows only makes matters worse: 'As a matter of fact he mistook the very nature of power. An exceptional man longs passionately to change something, to achieve something, and power comes to him; but Lawrence wanted power for the sake of the sensation, being far too unstable to have any dominating steady purpose.' That is simply false. From his first poems to his last 'pansies', Lawrence had a steady purpose—to find what the heart really believes in and what the heart really wants. All that is the metaphysical activity, the philosophizing, that Aldington despises. Lawrence did not despise it because he recognized that until the ground had been cleared of the rotten industrial civilization into which we have been born, there was no possibility of free scope for the artist. And how could the ground be cleared? Not in a day, to be sure, and not single handed. But by preaching in the wilderness, by revolutionary propaganda. That was Ruskin's idea, too, and Aldington is quite right in drawing a comparison between Lawrence and Ruskin (but not in asserting that Lawrence 'was the closer observer and the more vivid writer'). But he does this merely to assert that 'they shared an almost comical conviction of their power to change the world by writing a few books'. The world has been changed quite a bit since Aldington was born, and if he had had time to ask Lenin and Gandhi what caused them to be the chief agents of that change, he would have received the answer: 'a few books'—including some of Ruskin's!

Instead of deploring the waste of energy in Lawrence's 'vituperation and futile wrangling', let us rather be grateful that he was moved enough, angry enough, to rip the veil from our sham civilization, to expose its perversion and hypocrisy. What we must deplore is Lawrence's inability to keep calm, to build up a logical indictment, the effect—to use Bagehot's words again—'of his

deficiency in those masculine faculties—the reasoning understanding and firm far-seeing sagacity'. Neither Ruskin nor Lawrence
had the right temperamental disposition (perhaps not even the
crude physical strength) to effect that balance of emotion and reason
which alone can be fully persuasive. Even Tolstoy, a greater artist
than either of them, and a man built for the part, could not quite
pull it off. But when all this has been admitted and deplored, a very
real achievement remains. It may be that the main agent of our
changed and changing views about sex has been Freud. Freud
has seeped down into all sorts of popular channels, becoming
muddied in the process and often completely misunderstood. He is
a scientist and can be fully appreciated only by people with a
scientific training. But Lawrence had an intuitive recognition of
the truths revealed by Freud's analytical practice, and he fed this
intuition by wide reading in other directions—archaeology, mytho-
logy, anthropology, etc. I believe that in some respects he saw
farther and deeper than Freud, and his views on marital love and
on the education of children have a realism and originality which
most people are not yet ready to assimulate. On these questions he
was, to use the cant phrase, far in advance of his time.

In other words, Lawrence's ideas are not to be reconciled with
any existing social tendency, but that does not make them invalid:
it merely adds urgency to the need for a social change. Lawrence
was intelligent enough to see that the necessary social structure
would not be provided by 'democracy', and his contempt for the
political hypocrisy that goes by this name earned him the oppro-
bious taunt of 'fascist'. Lawrence was not a fascist: he was, if any
general name can be given to his highly individual views, a particular kind of anarchist—not my kind, but somewhere between
Tolstoy and Berdyaev. He had a deep loathing for the State and all
its works, and realized that salvation could only come spontaneously
from small communities. He dreamed of establishing such a community. He was drawn to the Etruscans because their evanescent
civilization seemed to have exhibited 'a real desire to preserve the
natural humour of life'. And far from being a fascist, he thought

that that was 'a task surely more worthy, and even much more difficult in the long run, than conquering the world or sacrificing the self or saving the immortal soul. Why,' he asked, 'has mankind such a craving to be imposed upon? Why this lust after imposing creeds, imposing deeds, imposing buildings, imposing language, imposing works of art? The thing becomes an imposition and a weariness at last. Give us things that are alive and flexible, which won't last too long and become an obstruction and a weariness.'

The real Lawrence, the 'basic' Lawrence, is in the words I have quoted, and in lines like these:*

> And I lift my head upon the troubled tangled
>   world, and though the pain
> Of living my life were doubled, I still have
>   this to comfort and sustain.
> I have such swarming sense of lives at the base
>   of me, such sense of lives
> Clustering upon me, reaching up, as each after
>   the other strives
> To follow my life aloft to the fine wild air of
>   life and the storm of thought,
> And though I scarcely see the boys, or know that
>   they are there, distraught
> As I am with living my life in earnestness, still
>   progressively and alone,
> Though they cling, forgotten the most part, not
>   companions, scarcely known
> To me—yet still because of the sense of their
>   closeness clinging densely to me,
> And slowly fingering up my stem and following, all
>   tinily
> The way that I have gone and now am leading, they
>   are dear to me.

* From 'The Schoolmaster', *Love Poems* London (Chatto & Windus), 1913.

That is the Lawrence who first moved me more than fifty years ago, and to whom I still feel grateful. It is not the Lawrence of Aldington's "Portrait"—'the world's rejected guest', 'the last of the Goliards', a man who was an artist in spite of himself, a genius, but . . . I do not believe that we can qualify genius in this particular way. It reminds me of the Marxist critic who has to admit the greatness of Tolstoy, *but* only on the assumption that all his ideas are 'historically necessary illusions'. The irregularity of Lawrence's genius—its inadequacy if you like—is patent, but as genius it is indivisible: the rough must be accepted with the smooth, the tough with the tender. Lawrence's ideas were tough, but they are not absurd, and they are not inconsistent with his poetic imagination. Aldington quotes Lawrence on Melville and thinks he has clinched his case:

Nobody can be more clownish, more clumsy and sententiously in bad taste. He preaches and holds forth because he is not sure of himself. And he holds forth, often, so amateurishly. The artist was so *much* greater than the man. The man is rather a tiresome New Englander of the ethical mystical-transcendentalist sort. But he was a deep, great artist, even if he was rather a sententious man . . . when he forgets his audience, and gives us his sheer appreciation of the world, then he is wonderful, his book commands a stillness in the soul, and awe.

But is Lawrence right about Melville? Is it not rather true, and part of the mystery of human nature, that only a particular kind of tension within a personality can produce a particular intensity of expression? Melville's ethical mystical-transcendentalism, I would say, was essential to the production of that wonderful 'stillness in the soul'. Only a genius capable of metaphysical speculation could have been aware of that particular 'awe' which he had the power to command. Only a Lawrence who had written the *Fantasia* would have been capable of writing that wonderful description of a religious procession in *Sea and Sardinia*, quoted by Aldington, or the last chapter of *Etruscan Places*. *Sons and Lovers*, *The Rainbow*, *The Plumed Serpent*, *The Man Who Died*, *Lady Chatterley's Lover*— these, the greatest and most typical of Lawrence's writings are not emanations of some pure aesthetic consciousness. They spring from a mental activity—a mind in revolt against the civilization it has inherited—and image and symbol, concept and intuition, fable and dogma, were smelted in the same burning brain. To attempt to dissociate two Lawrences is to betray his true significance.

The writer nearest to Lawrence is Whitman, as he himself realized. 'Whitman, the great poet, has meant so much to me. Whitman, the one man breaking a way ahead. Whitman, the one pioneer. And only Whitman.' And like Lawrence, Whitman raises the problem of the moral function of art. In his essay on Whitman Lawrence declares that 'the essential function of art is moral. Not aesthetic, not decorative, not pastime and recreation. But moral. The essential function of art is moral.' Aldington tries to save a decorative, an aesthetic Lawrence from the glorious confusion of his work. I can sympathize with his aim, for I have always myself fought against the deadening influence of moral judgement in art. But there is a difference between moral judgement and moral perception, and Lawrence knew it, and observed it. He continues, in his essay on Whitman: 'But a passionate, implicit morality, not didactic. A morality which changes the blood, rather than the mind. Changes the blood first. The mind follows later, in the wake. Now Whitman was a great moralist. He was a great leader. He was a great changer of the blood in the veins of men'. Admittedly this blood imagery is overworked by Lawrence, but he wanted to drive home the physical basis of sympathy, which is the clue to all aesthetic influence. Lawrence realized that art had grown dead on us, leprous and insentient. It has been killed by 'education'. 'To *force* the boy to see a correct one-eyed horse-profile is just like pasting a placard in front of his vision. It simply kills his inward seeing. We don't *want* him to see a proper horse. The child is *not* a little camera. He is a small vital organism which has direct dynamic *rapport* with the objects of the outer universe. He perceives from his breast and his

168

abdomen, with deep-sunken realism, the elemental nature of the creature.' And what is true of the child is true of the poet. Read the Preface to *New Poems* (reprinted in the Penguin *Essays*) for the clearest definition of Lawrence's aesthetic. He returns to Whitman. 'The quick of the universe is the *pulsating, carnal* self, mysterious and palpable . . . Because Whitman put this into his poetry, we fear him and respect him so profoundly . . . The utterance is like a spasm, naked contact with all influences at once. *It does not want to get anywhere* (my italics). It just takes place.' Who has ever heard of a morality that does not wish to get anywhere? But that is the kind of morality Lawrence was forever talking about: a somatic influence, a chemical transformation. The Greeks called it catharsis, but though Lawrence would not use such an academic word, he and Aristotle were talking about the same phenomenon: a purgation of the blood effected by the experience of great art.

To use the word 'art' in this context is to be reminded that Lawrence did not confine himself to the written word, the poetic image. All his life he wished to be a painter, too, and although it must be confessed that the only interest of the paintings that have survived is that they were painted by a genius whose natural medium of expression was the written word, yet they too emphasize the irregularity of his genius. If they were the only evidence of this man's attempt at creative expression, it is doubtful if they would have been preserved and given the lavish attention they now receive in various publications. This is not to say that they are completely lacking in artistic value; they have qualities of composition and of expressiveness that hold our attention and even stir our feelings. But these same qualities can be found in amateur paintings everywhere, and are not sufficient in themselves to constitute a work of art in the medium of oil or water-colour. Lawrence himself recognized that 'there are few, very few, great artists in any age. But there are hundreds and hundreds of men and women with genuine artistic talent and beautiful artistic feeling, who produce quite lovely works—not immortal, not masterpieces, not "great"; yet they are lovely, and will keep their loveliness a certain number of years; after which they will die, and the time will have to come to destroy them'.

I quote from *A Poet and Two Painters*, by Knud Merrild.* This book is by far the best, because the most professional and understanding, treatment of Lawrence as a painter. The work of a Danish painter who lived with his companion in a hut near Lawrence's at Taos in New Mexico in 1922–23, it is what Aldous Huxley at the time of its publication called 'perhaps the most vivid, the most objective and, one might say, the most distinguished portrait of Lawrence yet produced'. It is a faithful record of many conversations with Lawrence, but exasperating in as much as the author relies to a large extent on unspecified quotations from Lawrence's writings, with the following justification: 'If my book was to have any value at all, I must make it as accurate as possible. Then I remembered that Lawrence wrote as he spoke, wrote conversations down in his books or "talked" the thoughts and ideas in his books. What then could be more logical than to quote him direct from his books?' What, indeed? And since I find, in so far as I have been able to trace and check these quotations, that they are accurate, what could be 'more logical' than that I should quote direct from Mr Merrild's book?

Most of the paintings by Lawrence that have survived belong to the last four or five years of his life (1926–30). We find him writing to Dorothy Brett from Mablethorpe in Lincolnshire on 26 August, 1926; 'I'd paint, if I'd got paints, and could do it.' This mood seems to have been directly inspired by the East Anglian landscape— 'great sweeping sands that take the light, and little people that somehow seem lost in the light, and green sandhills'. But when, three months later, we hear from Florence of the first fruits of his resolve, it is a figure subject. 'I call it the "Unholy Family", because the *bambino*—with a *nimbus*—is just watching anxiously to see the young man give the semi-nude woman *un gros baiser. Molto moderno!*' Then follow, in rapid succession, such subjects as a

* London (Routledge), 1938.

'Boccaccio picture of the nuns and the gardener' and 'the third picture, the "Fight with an Amazon".'

Mrs Huxley had sent him a present of canvases, and it is to her that he reports his rapid progress. In February, 1927, he has just finished 'a nice big canvas, Eve dodging back into Paradise, between Adam and the Angel at the gate, who are having a fight about it, and leaving the world in flames in the far corner behind her. Great fun, and of course a *Capo lavoro!* I should like to do a middle picture, inside Paradise, just as she bolts in. God Almighty astonished and indignant, and the new young God who is just having a chat with the serpent, pleasantly amused, then the third picture, Adam and Eve under the tree of knowledge, God Almighty disappearing in a dudgeon, and the animals skipping.'

It continued for a while to be fun—'more fun and less soul-work than writing'—but in the Spring of this year Lawrence slackened off—perhaps on account of ill-health. He began a Resurrection, but we do not hear of any further activity until November, when he was 'still a bit groggy . . . but painting pictures of large and ruddy nymphs and fauns, to keep me in countenance'. In March, 1928, there is mention of 'a small canvas of a jaguar jumping on a man—*not* good, *not* finished, and I don't like it'. Then there is mention of 'three more water-colours; not bad, but I'd rather do oils: one can use one's elbows, and in water it's all dib-dab'. But now, too, there is the first mention of the possibility of holding an exhibition and by April 16th the plan has actualized—he is having his pictures shipped to London to be shown in the gallery owned by Dorothy Warren—'they might as well be shown. But I shan't sell them'. But before this he had painted several other subjects—on April 2nd there is mention of seven more water-colours, "Adam Throwing the Apple", "The Mango Tree", "The Torch Dance", "Yawning", "The Lizard", "Under the Haystack" and ' . . . a charming picture of a man pissing . . . called "Dandelions", for short. Now I'm doing a small thing in oil, called "The Rape of the Sabine Women" or "A Study in Arses".' In this letter he disclaims any intention of selling the paintings, but 'if I sell my novel,

I might reproduce them in a portfolio, and sell that—500 copies'.

The "Finding of Moses" and a "Family in Garden" are mentioned on April 25th—the first 'really fine negresses' and the second 'rather small—all nude, of course—me in hammock, pa on his heels squatting, and two *bambini*.' In a letter to Mark Gertler on May 24th he mentions 'seven big pictures—oils—a "Nymphs and Faun", all dark orange . . . Also a "Fight with an Amazon" ' (perhaps the one mentioned earlier); and he again expresses his own preference for oils. Later in 1928 (August) he mentions in a letter to Harry Crosby 'a nice canvas of sun-fauns and sun-nymphs laughing at the Crucifixion—but I had to paint out the Crucifixion'. In the same letter he informs Crosby that he is to have an exhibition in London in October and probably in New York in November, in Alfred Stieglitz's gallery. Other items referred to in this same letter are 'a little painting I did of men catching sun-horses—quite tiny' and 'a drawing of the Sun, from a maya design' which he enclosed as a gift to Crosby ('You can blank out the lettering if you like.'). In September he wrote to Enid Hilton (who acted as a go-between with the Warren Gallery) about 'the picture *Contadini* . . . two Italian peasants, as the word itself says'.

The paintings destined for exhibition in London were 'yielded up' to Dorothy Warren during the course of July, 1920, but the opening of the show was postponed owing to the excitement and risk of prosecution attending the publication of *Lady Chatterley's Lover*. Copies of this book had been confiscated by the police and Lawrence feared 'they'd follow up by confiscating the pictures'. He instructed Dorothy Warren to choose her own time and meanwhile have the pictures photographed, for eventual reproduction. The idea of a portfolio amused him very much.

The exhibition was finally opened at the Warren Gallery on June 15th, 1921, and was an immediate success. Complaints of its indecency were made to the Home Office and on July 5th, three weeks after the opening, Detective-Inspector Gordon Hester and Detective-Sergeant Thomas descended on the Gallery with six policemen and took away thirteen of the paintings. Lawrence was alarmed for the fate of his pictures and wrote to Dorothy Warren (from Italy) on July 14th to beg her to compromise with the police rather than allow them to be burned: 'There is something sacred to me about my pictures, and I will not have them burnt, for all the liberty of England. I am an Englishman, and I do my bit for the liberty of England. But I am most of all a man, and my first creed is that my manhood and my sincere utterance shall be inviolate and beyond nationality or any other limitation. To admit that my pictures should be burned, in order to change an English law, would be to admit that sacrifice of life to circumstances which I most strongly disbelieve in'.

The paintings were eventually restored to Dorothy Warren, but what happened to them afterwards remains somewhat of a mystery. They were dispersed. It was only in 1964, more than forty years after the event, that an attempt was made to reassemble the paintings exhibited in 1921, and to survey the whole range of Lawrence's painting activity.* It is amazing to find how much of it there was, and how greatly the activity mattered to Lawrence. Indeed, one must now conclude that any complete understanding of Lawrence as a writer is not possible unless one takes into account his work as a painter. Both activities, though so far separated in the value of the achievement, were an integral part of his genius.

Why did Lawrence suddenly begin to paint about the age of forty? It is not strictly true to say that he only began to paint at this age because he had always from boyhood wanted 'to make pictures'. Merrild tells us that he had been 'making drawings and water-colours for many years, and at some time he had made a copy of Piero di Cosimo's *Death of Procris* (in the National Gallery, London). Presumably Lawrence worked from a print and he carried this copy about with him on his travels—he had it with him in New Mexico. Merrild and his friend Gótzsche thought it was very amateurish, 'the colour muddy and the drawing helplessly but

---

* *Paintings of D. H. Lawrence.* Texts by Harry T. Moore, Jack Lindsay and Herbert Read. London (Cory, Adams & Mackay), 1964. The substance of my contribution is embodied in this essay.

painfully done, seemingly in great earnestness'. He confessed to
Merrild that he had had only one real lesson in painting in his life,
and had early decided he could not draw. 'When I did paint jugs
of flowers or bread and potatoes, or cottages in a lane, copying from
nature, the result wasn't very thrilling. Nature was nore or less of
a plaster-cast to me—those plaster-cast heads of Minerva or figures
of dying gladiators which so unnerved me as a youth. The "object",
be it what it might, was always slightly repulsive to me, once I sat
down in front of it, to paint it. So, of course, I decided I couldn't
paint. Perhaps I can't. But I verily believe I can make pictures,
which is to me all that matters in this respect. The art of painting
consists of making pictures—and so many artists accomplish
canvases without coming within miles of painting a picture.'*

'Making pictures' seems for a long time to have meant for
Lawrence copying his favourite masterpieces from the past. He
kept a small portfolio of coloured prints, chiefly of Renaissance and
primitive Italian paintings. There seems to be something quite
naïve in this approach to the practice of the art, but Lawrence had
no inhibitions about it. 'I learned to paint from copying other
pictures—usually reproductions, sometimes even photographs.
When I was a boy how I concentrated over it! Copying some
perfectly worthless reproduction in some magazine. I worked with
almost dry water-colour, stroke by stroke, covering half a square
inch at a time, each inch perfect and complete, proceeding in a kind
of mosaic advance, with no idea at all of laying on a broad wash.
Hours and hours of intense concentration, inch by inch progress,
in a method entirely wrong—and yet these copies of mine managed,
when they were finished, to have a certain something that delighted
me—a certain glow of life, which was beauty to me.' His copy of
Greiffenhagen's *Idyll* perhaps illustrates Lawrence's sentimental
approach to beauty, but by the time he painted the *Fight with an
Amazon* (an almost identical composition) the idyll had been
luridly transformed.

He relates how he became more ambitious and went on to copy

* Merrild, *op. cit.*, p. 210.

the English water-colourists from a series of reproductions issued by *The Studio* in eight parts, and in this difficult enterprise he 'not only acquired a considerable technical skill in handling water-colour . . . but also I developed visionary awareness'. He confesses (in contradiction to his statements at other times) that paint 'gave me a form of delight that words can never give. Perhaps the joy in words goes deeper and is for that reason more unconscious. The *conscious* delight is certainly stronger in paint'.

But all this delight is evoked by copying, and bad as the copies seem to have been (according to Merrild, 'his work possessed no interest whatsoever as a work of painting and would not attract any attention among thousands of mediocre copies'), there is no doubt that Lawrence was obsessed by the activity, and that it had profound significance for him. Even Merrild admits that his work had an interest as an expression of the man himself. The copies were even full of errors that were characteristic. For example, in the copy of *The Death of Procris*, a picture which Merrild knew very well, Lawrence had painted the blood that flows from the body a vivid red, quite out of key with the rest of the composition. When this was pointed out to him Lawrence admitted that the variation was deliberate. 'I delighted so in painting that bloodstream. I could not resist the urge to make it real red-red, only I couldn't get it bloody enough, the warm, slightly steaming, liquid red blood. I wanted to experience the lust of killing in that picture. Killing is natural to man, you know. It is just as natural as lying with a woman. I often feel I could kill and enjoy it.'

In that statement, which is authentic Lawrence, he betrays, if not his complete misunderstanding of the art of painting, then an obstinate will to abuse the art for his own literary purposes. Lawrence was an expressionist, an extreme example of that type of artist who seeks a direct correspondence between feeling and representation, to the neglect of the more sophisticated values of proportion and harmony.

In Taos Lawrence had often watched Merrild painting and had become fascinated and envious. On one occasion he tried to snatch the brush out of Merrild's hand in order to paint part of the picture. Merrild had to struggle with him to get the brush back. He does not seem to have painted any pictures in New Mexico, but obviously he had been inspired by the example of the Danish painter and when he began to paint in earnest three years later, he no longer 'made a picture' but painted as (in the "Introduction to these Paintings" he said an artist should paint) with his whole consciousness—'that form of complete consciousness in which predominates the intuitive awareness of forms, images, the *physical* awareness'.

When, in the autumn of 1926, he found that he was self-confident enough to embark on his own original composition, he became a typical expressionist, like Nolde or Soutine. But without, alas, the sensuous harmony of the one or the pulsating rhythm of the other. But Lawrence did achieve the quality that he himself most desired, vitality. In spite of his literary approach and his technical inadequacy, one can admit that every picture *lives*—lives, as he said, 'with the life you put into it. If you put no *life* into it—no thrill, no concentration of delight or passion of visual discovery—then the picture is dead, like so many canvases, no matter how much thorough and scientific work is put into it . . . It needs a certain purity of spirit to be an artist, of any sort.'

And that was Lawrence's own decisive quality, in his writing as well as in his painting. 'An artist may be a profligate and, from the social point of view, a scoundrel. But if he can paint a nude woman, or a couple of apples, so that they are a living image, then he is pure in spirit, and, for the time being, his is the kingdom of heaven. This is the beginning of all art, visual or literary or musical: be pure in spirit.'

Art, for Lawrence, was a form of religion. 'Art is a form of supremely delicate awareness and atonement—meaning at-one-ness, the state of being one with the object—a great atonement in delight, for I can never look on art as a form of delight.'

'The curious delight in image-making'—it is a human instinct, coeval with the human race, and Lawrence, least of all men, could not deny himself that delight. Any value there is in his paintings is not artistic, nor even biographical, but moral. They challenge us to cast off our own inhibitions and experience a similar delight.

Not immortal, not masterpieces, not 'great', not even 'lovely', but these paintings will not die so soon as Lawrence himself might have wished; for they are visual evidence of the struggle of a great spirit to liberate himself from

> the darkened spaces
> Of fear, and of frightened spaces

and return, 'back beyond good and evil', to

> the angel-guarded
> Gates of the long-discarded
> Garden, which God has hoarded
> Against our pain.

XI

Edwin Muir

If I begin by speaking of myself in this brief memoir of Edwin Muir it is because I was always aware of a deep affinity of origins and experience, and this may be my best qualification for writing about such a man. We had both been born on remote farms, and though Orkney is a long way from North-East Yorkshire, they were both Viking or Scandinavian settlements and the place-names that echoed in our infant ears have a striking similarity. Wyre and Wass, Ness and Garth. In the farmyard our sensibilities had been assailed by the same elemental sights and smells, though I had no experience of the sea. The parallel does not end with childhood. At the age of fifteen we had both gone to large industrial cities to become clerks at the same salary of four shillings and twopence a week. But then after a few years our careers began to diverge. Muir's experience in Glasgow was grim, and lasted for eighteen years; mine in Leeds was more genteel and lasted for only three years. I was ambitious and resolved to better myself. Muir remained unambitious to the end of his life, and more reluctantly than anyone I have ever known, had his greatness thrust upon him.

During our youth we had experienced the same intellectual excitements, acquiring our knowledge from public libraries and cheap books bought with the few pennies we managed to save. We were both swept away by Nietzsche, who became the guide to our further education. We both became interested in Guild Socialism, read *The New Age*, and eventually contributed to its pages. We both came under the influence of its editor, A. R. Orage—a man of great

intelligence and intuitive understanding, who naturally attracted
disciples, as Muir said of him. But there the parallel ends, for the
First World War had meanwhile broken out and I was caught up in
it. Muir escaped because his physique was not equal to it. It plays
little part in his *Autobiography*, whereas in my life it is the water-
shed that divides innocence from experience, faith from disillusion,
hope from frustration. For this reason Muir could always attend
and listen to a class of experiences to which the war had left me
sardonically indifferent. He describes these experiences in his
autobiography:

The experiences I mean are of little practical use and have no
particular economic or political interest. They come when I am
least aware of myself as a personality moulded by my will and time;
in moments of contemplation when I am unconscious of my body,
or indeed that I have a body with separate members; in moments
of grief or prostration; in happy hours with friends; and, because
self-forgetfulness is most complete then, in dreams and daydreams
and in that floating, half-discarnate state which precedes and
follows sleep. In these hours there seems to me to be knowledge of
my real self and simultaneously knowledge of immortality.

I have never had such experiences and to me a belief in immortality
remains in substance a convenient myth.

In discussing Orage, and contrasting him with another friend
who was very close to him, Muir draws a distinction between a
personality, such as Orage was, and what after Goethe he can only
call a 'nature':

A personality is too obviously the result of a collaboration between
its owner and Time, too clearly *made*; and no matter how fascinating
or skilful the workmanship may be, ultimately it bores us. Orage
was much more than a personality, but he kept that 'more' to himself
as if jealously guarding his real strength, and it was his personality

that he turned to the world; he was too proud of it. Holms had hardly any personality at all; when he impressed you it was by pure, uncontaminated power . . . To show the irreducible second-rateness of a man of personality one has only to think of Holms's words in his letter to Hugh Kingsmill: 'The supreme height of individual self-expression, and union with the universe, are one.' If the soul is immortal and the personality is not, obviously our real task is not to cultivate but to get rid of personality.

This distinction is a clue to Muir's own life, which was so gentle and self-effacing, and impressed his friends with almost a sense of holiness. His poetry is unified by this quality in his character and experience. Muir did not begin to write poetry until he was thirty-five, and the public has been slow to recognize its virtues. It is not the poetry of any school; its diction is cautious and unassertive. Nevertheless it progressed intensively and is now a body of verse that challenges comparison with the work of any of his contemporaries. In historical perspective it may seem to be the natural continuation of the poetry of Yeats.

In our present state of deprivation we must guard against sentimental exaggeration. Muir rarely conveys the immediate excitement that we associate with the later Yeats, nor does he evoke our spiritual predicament with the vivid poignancy of the early Eliot. He is not a magical poet; sometimes he is pedestrian. But if he is pedestrian he is always marching on the fixed point of a precise vision, and his poetry is therefore accumulative in its force; one has to read it as one reads a Book of Hours, or a chain of meditations. Perhaps the *Centuries* of Traherne is the nearest comparison, and we know that Muir had a great fondness for Traherne. Muir's is not metaphysical poetry, in the academic sense; it is not conceitful. The imagery is bland, the metaphors simple and not contrived. Sometimes, as in "The Horses", the imagination is Yeatsian in its cosmic scope; but more often it is humble, of conversational ease, in the manner of George Herbert:

They could not tell me who should be my lord,
But I could read from every word they said
The common thought: Perhaps that lord was dead,
And only a story now and a wandering word.
How could I follow a word or serve a fable,
They asked me, 'Here are lords a-plenty. Take
Service with one, if only for your sake;
Yet better be your own master if you're able.'

I would rather scour the roads, a masterless dog,
Than take such service, be a public fool,
Obstreperous or tongue-tied, a good rogue,
Than be with those, the clever and the dull,
Who say that lord is dead; when I can hear
Daily his dying whisper in my ear.

Such simplicity easily falls into banality; but it can also rise into
the purest beauty, as it does in "Day and Night", especially in this
first verse:

I wrap the blanket of the night
About me, fold on fold on fold—
And remember how as a child
Lost in the newness of the light
I first discovered what is old
From the night and the soft night wind.
For in the daytime all was new,
Moving in light and in the mind
All at once, thought, shape, and hue.
Extravagant novelty too wild
For the new eyes of a child.

The sentiment is not original—it is Traherne's; and the opening
metaphor is a Yeatsian cliché; yet how naturally, and how inevitably
the accents fall.

I think there is another poet who must have influenced Muir, though I do not remember any reference to him—Coventry Patmore. There are certain later poems, such as "The Late Wasp" and "The Late Swallow", that have Patmore's well-wrought cadence; but the comparison ends on the technical level—no two poets could have had such different 'natures'.

The *Collected Poems* will have to be revised now, and brought to a sad conclusion. May we hope also for a volume of Collected Essays? This, too, would be impressive. Again of no school, grinding no academic axe, the criticism is yet firm and profound, and of remarkable range. There must be many scattered essays that have never been republished; I remember one that impressed me very much at the time of its publication on "Calvin and Marx". Muir was not politically-minded. I like to think that he was a fellow anarchist:

What I believe in is a modest, peaceable life in this world, a faulty, forgiving, on the whole happy life, where no man can exploit his neighbour and people work together in a friendly way and die when their time comes; a life which cannot be right unless its relation to the heavens is right. It is the universal frame overarching and embracing everything that gives meaning and proportion to the whole.

In all his work, especially his poetry, Muir was obsessed with Time. In the "Extracts from a Diary" printed at the end of *The Story and the Fable* (the original version of *An Autobiography*), he describes this obsession humorously:

I was born before the Industrial Revolution, and am now about two hundred years old. But I have skipped a hundred and fifty of them. I was really born in 1737, and till I was fourteen no time-accidents happened to me. Then in 1751 I set out from Orkney to Glasgow. When I arrived I found it was not 1751, but 1901, and that a hundred and fifty years had been burned up in my two days' journey. But I myself was still in 1751, and remained there for a long time. All my life I have been trying to overhaul that invisible leeway.

Edwin Muir has now caught up with time and for him the riddle is solved: he is at peace. He found the perfect expression of his faith (he disclaimed the word philosophy) in the *Upanishads*, in the doctrine of the Self—the Self 'that is not known through discourse, splitting of hairs, learning however great. He comes to the man He loves; takes that man's body as His own . . .', for his sake makes the Word flesh. In one of his finest poems, "The Incarnate One", he speaks of the 'ideological instruments' that have betrayed the natural man, and warns us that:

> The fleshless word, growing, will bring us down,
> Pagan and Christian man alike will fall,
> The auguries say, the white and black and brown,
> The merry and sad, theorist, lover, all
> Invisibly will fall:
> Abstract calamity, save for those who can
> Build their cold empire on the abstract man.
>
> A soft breeze stirs and all my thoughts are blown
> Far out to sea and lost. Yet I know well
> The bloodless word will battle for its own
> Invisibly in brain and nerve and cell.
> The generations tell
> Their personal tale: the One has far to go
> Past the mirages and the murdering snow.

To proclaim one's faith in the incarnate One is to assert the superiority of the *vita contemplativa* in a world devoted to meaningless work and desperate erethism. Muir's significance is the significance of a dedicated man of letters, and his life of devotion is a silent criticism not only of the conventional notion of success (which confuses art with entertainment), but also of those more professional betrayals which take the form of wilful eccentricity, abstract speculation, or intellectual snobbery (as Mr Cyril Connolly would say, 'he never belonged to the literary élite').

I do not think Muir felt very optimistic about the survival of his values in our doomed civilization. But his imagination reached beyond this historical moment, to the cosmic revolution that astrologers predict, that Yeats saw in vision, and that even to more rational philosophers now seems inevitable and imminent.